WAS IT WORTH IT?

HOW TO CREATE YOUR OWN

PURPOSEFUL PARENTING PLAN

WAS IT WORTH IT?

CAROL JEAN WILSON ALLEN

NOTE: This book offers guidance based on the author's personal experiences. It is not intended to replace professional psychological, financial, legal, or other expert advice. If professional assistance is required, readers are encouraged to consult a qualified and trusted expert.

All photos are from the author's personal collection.

Copyright © 2025 by Carol Jean Wilson Allen

All rights reserved. No part of this book may be reproduced in any manner whatsoever without written permission except in the case of brief quotations embodied in critical articles and reviews.

Hardcover ISBN: 9781950544554
EBook ISBN: 9781950544561

Rand-Smith Publishing

First Printing, 2025

DEDICATION

I would like to thank my husband, Chris Allen, who had faith in my ability and encouraged me to write this book. In memory of my parents, grandparents, and brother, I am forever grateful for the life they gave me and the memories that I will always have.

Contents

1	Introduction	1
2	What Is a Purposeful Parenting Plan?	5
3	My Story	11
4	Know Thy Self	29
5	Develop the Plan	39
6	Execute the Plan	51
7	Lessons in Parenting	63
8	Collect Feedback	125
9	The Evolution of Parenting Styles	133
10	Generational Parenting Styles	139
11	Performing a Self-Evaluation	149
12	Managing the Hand We're Dealt	157
13	Lessons Learned	161
14	Was It Worth It?	165

Epilogue	175
Acknowledgements	179
About the Author	181

1

Introduction

Over the years, I have received numerous comments from colleagues and acquaintances urging me to document my journey as a parent. They often reference the somewhat unique methods I used and how my two daughters have turned out, frequently saying, "The apple doesn't fall far from the tree." My story is one of resilience and determination, shaped by nearly a quarter-century of single parenthood.

Research clearly shows that single-parent households typically face more challenges than those with two parents, and that's not even considering factors like race, income, and social status, which can create additional issues. Despite these challenges, through unwavering dedication and a clear parenting strategy, I have successfully guided my daughters toward what is often regarded as "success."

My elder daughter, Candice, excelled in school. She thrived in academic and extracurricular activities, from music to athletics. Today, she is an accomplished lawyer, having quickly risen to the position of senior legal counsel at a globally recognized company. Additionally, she is happily married and the mother of two children.

Danielle, my younger daughter, showed leadership potential from a young age. Her achievements span academics, music, sports, and dance. Currently, she holds the position of Sr. Vice President at a school district, building upon her significant contributions at Teach for America, an education non-profit organization.

I like to believe that my approach to parenting paved the way for their success, as that was always my goal and singular focus. Throughout my journey as a parent, I spent countless nights contemplating the best ways to raise my daughters. My approach was organized and disciplined, as I meticulously planned each step.

I hope to share some of those methods with you in this book. I developed the Purposeful Parenting Plan (PPP) to encapsulate this approach. Although they are primarily parenting strategies, they are also life lessons that can benefit people of all ages.

This narrative draws on a blend of renowned behavioral theories and my personal observations and insights, incorporating my interpretation of the thoughts of Freud, Pavlov, Piaget, Skinner, Thorndike, Maslow, and Dr. Spock, who all provided valuable insights during my children's formative years.

My plan outlines four overarching strategies based on my experiences. As you learn more about this method, I invite you to create your own PPP. My hope is that this will enable you to embrace the journey of raising children while also taking care of yourself.

As a matter of principle, I aim to respect the privacy of individuals and institutions, focusing on experiences rather than specific names. These experiences, both rewarding and challenging, shaped me into the person I am today.

In preparation for this book, I reflected on how my parents raised me and the lessons I learned from them. I also "interviewed" my daughters about their childhood memories and asked for their feedback on my parenting style. I knew this would be very informative and welcomed it as an opportunity to continue learning and growing.

Their reflections affirmed my unique approach to their upbringing. They often emphasized how well-prepared they felt for life's challenges and attributed much of this to my guidance. Our conversations, which began virtually due to the pandemic, were filled with humor and fond nostalgia. Whether their feedback was positive or not, these discussions only strengthened our bond.

Now, as a grandmother and the wife of my second husband, I continue to be a guiding force for the next generation. My family, consisting of my daughters, their father, their children and significant others, my husband, and his children and grandchildren, coexist harmoniously.

Through deliberate actions and thoughtful decisions, you, too, can create a nurturing environment that allows your children to grow and flourish. As they mature into adults, you will experience a profound sense of fulfillment, knowing that you played a significant role in shaping their futures.

By following the approaches outlined in this book, I hope you will embark on the rewarding adventure of raising children, confident in the knowledge that you are doing your absolute best.

Candice and Danielle are living their best lives

2

What Is a Purposeful Parenting Plan?

Before you start writing anything down, you should learn the PPP concepts so that you can apply them as you go along. I've broken them down into four areas. Once you understand this section, you will be ready to begin preparing your plan.

The four approaches of the **Purposeful Parenting Plan:**

1. Know Thyself
2. Develop the Plan
3. Execute the Plan
4. Get Feedback

First, I'll provide a general description of each step, and then in the next few chapters, we will go into more depth on why I created this method and how it can help you on your parenting journey.

Know Thyself

Let me tell you, this is the most crucial work you'll ever do as a parent – and it's not something you can skim through. It's time to take a deep dive into yourself. No holding back! But don't worry; this isn't about being critical or judgmental. It starts with being genuine and honest about who you are and how you got here.

So, let's strip away any blame or finger-pointing—you are who you are, and that's what we will uncover. This private journey is all about figuring out how you handle life's curveballs, how you tackle the highs and lows, and what truly makes you tick.

There is no need to share this with anyone; it's your introspective adventure. Think about it – are you the kind of person who cherishes a solid twelve-hour snooze or thrives on just five hours of sleep? Do you crave nourishing, healthy meals or indulge in some delicious junk food? Are you a social butterfly, or do you savor your moments of solitude? Or all the above?

Let's dive even more deeply. What lights up your soul and brings a tear to your eye? Are you a carefree, free spirit or more comfortable with structured routines?

Knowing all this is like discovering the treasure map to your method of successful parenting. When you understand yourself, you can uncover the best way to raise your children in a way that resonates with who you are at your core.

So, get ready for this thrilling self-discovery journey. Embrace it, enjoy it, and get to know the fantastic person you are – the parent extraordinaire!

Develop the Plan

How did I develop my Purposeful Parenting Plan? When my friend said, "I just put one foot in front of the other" while raising kids, it got me thinking. Sure, it's a journey filled with surprises. Still, I've found that having things thought out in advance is the key to reliable and successful parenting. And guess what? The sooner you know yourself, the better you can shape that PPP to match your reality.

As a healthcare administrator, I created strategic plans for medical facilities. I quickly learned the power of having a vision, setting goals, and defining objectives for success. It's like building a mission statement that guides your actions every step of the way. And let me tell you, using a SWOT analysis (Strengths, Weaknesses, Opportunities, Threats) and exploring various scenarios were essential in crafting those plans. I realized that the same principles apply to being successful in life, including parenting.

You see, knowing your strengths and weaknesses is fundamental. Even Superman had his Kryptonite! Recognizing areas where you might need support and delegating those tasks to people who can handle them better is essential. Parenting is a team effort, after all!

But it doesn't stop there. We must identify the opportunities available to us and always be aware of potential threats. Life is full of obstacles, and we must equip ourselves to manage or even overcome them. Imagine applying the principles you've learned throughout your life and the wisdom gathered from observing others to become the best parent you can be. It's like taking all that valuable knowledge from school and those classes you attended and putting it into purposeful action: a Purposeful Parenting Plan!

So, let's embark on this thrilling adventure of self-discovery and strategic planning for parenting. Embrace your strengths, be open about your weaknesses, and gather your needed support and knowledge. With a well-prepared PPP and a lot of love, we'll navigate this parenting journey like the superheroes we truly are!

Execute the Plan

This is the real deal, the moment of truth! The most challenging yet most crucial work lies ahead. I'm talking about implementing that well-crafted plan you've developed – from the moment your little one arrives until they reach a minimum age of eighteen or twenty-one.

This is where you put your goals and objectives into action, day in and day out, week after week, month after month, and year after year.

It might seem daunting initially, but it gets easier with time. Once you settle into the groove, you'll reap the rewards as both a person and a parent. Following your PPP is the key to smoother child-rearing and a more predictable journey.

You've worked hard to know yourself inside out and created a comprehensive PPP that aligns with your vision as a parent. It's time to embrace the challenge, roll up your sleeves, and get things done. Each day brings new opportunities to shape your child's future, and you've got this!

Remember, you're in the driver's seat, confidently steering your family toward a fulfilling and purposeful life. As you travel toward your goals, you get closer to success, your ultimate destination. Stay committed to your PPP, and watch the magical journey unfold.

So, let's hit the ground running! You can positively impact your child's life – and that's something to be genuinely proud of. Keep going, keep growing, and relish every moment of this incredible parenting adventure. You've laid the groundwork, and now it's time to shine!

Collect Feedback

Here's the ultimate key to unlocking the truth about our parenting journey: ask our children! It's time to have those candid conversations and get some real, solid insights into how they felt about their upbringing and how they turned out. Of course, the key is to raise them to be honest, and then they will give you honest feedback.

Believe me, their candid answers will give us all the information we need to gauge our performance as parents. It's like a report card on our parenting skills! If they're open to discussing their childhood with you, it's a great sign that you've done something right. More groundwork must be done if there's any hesitation, anger, or avoidance.

Now, I know there are plenty of other influences and variables in their lives, but let's focus on what we can control. My kids are adults now, and I couldn't help but wonder about the impact of all my time, effort, and sacrifices. So, I decided to have these conversations at a time that suited both them and me.

Timing matters, folks! After their teenage years, completing their education, landing jobs, and starting their own families, they've gained a more mature outlook on life. So, it's the perfect time to have those heartfelt talks.

Video meetings can work wonders if they don't live close by or if they have busy schedules but plan the sessions well in advance. Let your children know what the meeting is for – honest evaluations of your parenting techniques. It's all about creating a safe space where they can share openly...and you are prepared to receive.

Here's the real deal: Listen with an open heart and mind during these conversations. No judgment, no arguments. Just soak in their words and actions, both spoken and unspoken. When you are ready, ask questions to understand their perspective better.

Remember, our goal is growth and development for our children and ourselves. So, let's put our parenting skills to the test and find out how we can do even better. Together, we'll shape the future with love, understanding, and a willingness to learn. Onward to heart-to-heart conversations and building stronger bonds with our amazing kids!

Family gathering at 10th wedding anniversary of Chris and me

3

My Story

Before we get into the nuts and bolts of creating your own Purposeful Parenting Plan, let me share a bit about my background so you can understand my journey. This is important because, as you will soon learn, the first step in creating a powerful PPP is to reflect on your background, experiences, and upbringing.

Self-reflection is difficult. It's challenging work, so sharing my story might help you feel more comfortable examining your situation. The goal is to understand your path, parenting influences, and lessons you've learned along the way. You can then use those unique life experiences to build a solid foundation for your plan.

Background

My story traces back to the diverse heritage that shaped who I am today. From stories passed down, I learned that my ancestors endured the brutalities of slavery in the South before the year 1865. On my father's side, his parents sought opportunities in the coal mines of Girard, Kansas, while my mother's family hails from the vibrant state of Tennessee. My great-grandparents on my mother's side were well-educated, operating a licensed funeral home in Missouri, laying the groundwork for their legacy, a rare opportunity for African Americans at that time.

My father, a high school history teacher, was the thirteenth of fourteen children from a farming family where the older sons toiled in the coal mines. He was quite intelligent, and I vividly remember sitting in awe as he aced almost every question on *Jeopardy*. Those gentle moments spent together watching the show etched unforgettable memories in my heart.

My mother met my father in Webster Groves, Missouri. Both college graduates with postgraduate degrees paved the way for a loving and nurturing environment for my brother and me. My mother, an exceptional cook, also dedicated herself to the family's funeral home business, where unique experiences awaited us.

Given their line of work, my brother Charles and I had a rather unconventional childhood, to say the least! Charles answered the phone at the tender age of four, and I played with my dolls in the embalming room when I was just two years old. It was quite an experience! Who knows how these early encounters shaped us, but I can tell you one interesting fact—I eventually developed an allergy to formaldehyde, a substance commonly used in embalming fluid.

Ah, the funeral home! It was a place where emotions ran raw and deep. Every day, people from all walks of life arrived, grief-stricken, screaming, fainting, and crying. It was a space where I witnessed humanity's best and worst. I realized early on that death spared no one; it could come at any age, through any means, and it was final. This stark realization made me value life even more, motivating me to strive to be the best version of myself, to leave a legacy in my community, and to extend a helping hand to those less fortunate.

My wise grandmother, the matriarch of the funeral business, instilled in me the importance of giving back and working diligently for what matters most. As a family, we embraced hard work—while my father was a teacher, my grandmother, mother, brother, and I were all relentless students in academics and the family business.

During my teenage years, I spent most summer days in a room at the funeral home, diligently completing paperwork while softly listening to the radio. It was a testament to the work ethic I learned from working in the family business, which has served me exceptionally well throughout my life.

The Path I Chose

Childhood memories are those cherished moments that leave an everlasting impact on who we become. When I was thirteen, my family moved to a quaint little private block on a dead-end street, creating the backdrop for some of my fondest recollections. It was an idyllic neighborhood filled with multi-ethnic families, and we were a tight-knit community where I had fun and enjoyed genuine camaraderie.

Our neighborhood was a haven for laughter and joy. We'd spend our days playing together, organizing epic street parties that brought all the families out of their houses. It was a time when the world felt safe, and the kids could ride their bikes freely without any traffic woes or other dangers. Those carefree days still fill me with warmth and nostalgia; they are some of my best childhood memories.

Surrounded by friends and with loving parents, I couldn't have asked for a better start in life. My mother ensured we always had healthy meals on the table. She was a hard worker, and I admired her dedication and tenacity, which would later influence my work ethic. My father was a wellspring of wisdom and knowledge. We spent countless summer days engrossed in playing games like cards and croquet. And then, there were those unforgettable midnight movie sessions where he'd wake me up to watch his favorite old films. Those moments were magical, and to this day, watching old movies brings back the fondest memories of my father, whom I miss dearly. During those cherished movie nights, I found solace, and they became a lifelong comfort, especially when raising my two girls.

But let me take you back to a pivotal day on our street, where everything changed. The neighborhood kids were enjoying their usual routine, putting on plays in garages, running, biking, and having a blast. Then, suddenly, a commotion erupted near the end of the street. Curiosity got the better of us, and we rushed to witness the source of the turmoil—two sisters engaged in a heated altercation.

Verbal and physical attacks filled the air as they vented their frustrations for all to see. It was a baffling sight: two sisters I assumed loved each other dearly, airing their grievances in the street. I couldn't wrap my head around their actions. Why expose their disagreements to the world? Why not settle matters in the privacy of their home?

That incident affected me deeply. It left me pondering human behavior and the underlying motivations that drive people to act the way they do. It sparked an insatiable curiosity, and I longed to understand why individuals behaved counterproductively to their goals.

Of course, working in a funeral home provided me with other examples of perplexing behavior. I witnessed firsthand how some relatives, who hadn't been part of their loved one's life for years, suddenly felt entitled to make decisions without contributing anything meaningful. Their actions only added sadness and stress to the already grieving family. I wondered why people yearned to be included, yet their actions alienated those they claimed to love.

Those puzzling observations of human nature, like fighting in the street and the eye-opening reactions to challenging behavior during a funeral, sparked a deep desire to learn and understand. I knew I wanted to delve into the intricacies of human thought and behavior. Then, I realized psychology was my calling and eagerly awaited college to pursue my passion. That incident set me on a fascinating journey of understanding the human mind.

Parental Influences

In the tapestry of my life, I was fortunate to be woven into a two-parent home that laid the groundwork for who I am today. My father, born eleven years before my mother, emerged from a large rural family, while my mother, an only child, grew up in the bustling city. Their unique backgrounds shaped their parenting styles, and their harmonious union instilled a sense of stability and strength in me.

With his indirect parenting style, my father had a way with words, using them judiciously to correct or discipline me. On the other hand, my mother was more direct, having clear expectations of how I should conduct myself as a young lady. Together, they embraced an authoritative style of parenting, widely recognized for its effectiveness in nurturing children in a positive environment.

My early years as an only child ended when my brother, Charles, entered our lives. Like any typical older sibling, I wasn't thrilled about sharing the spotlight, and I jokingly asked my mother to send him back to where he came from. Of course, I wasn't serious, but I had to adjust to having a sibling and the occasional feeling of being dethroned. Charles was a charming and charismatic addition to the family, blessed with leadership qualities and boundless energy. However, I couldn't help but notice that he often seemed to enjoy more leniency than I did, much to my chagrin.

Life as the older sibling meant fighting for everything, while Charles seemingly breezed through life without a care. He had a talent for slipping out of trouble, and sometimes, I would find myself unfairly blamed for his antics. However, my brother and I shared a deep bond, and I loved him dearly despite the occasional rivalry. I always knew he would play a significant role in the family business, and his leadership qualities were evident early on. He became the class president in high school, a testament to his magnetic personality.

Upon reflection, our family life was serene, with love and laughter prevailing over discord and strife. We worked hard and relished life's little moments whenever possible. One admirable aspect of my parents and their relationship was their conscious effort to shield my brother and me from any disagreements they may have had. Occasionally, they'd mention a "family discussion" with my grandmother, a discreet way of acknowledging issues without exposing us to unpleasant arguments. This disciplined approach left a lasting impression on me, for I believed then, as I do now, that seeing parents argue can be distressing.

Nothing was more upsetting to me than the rare instance when I'd see my parents having disagreements, no matter how insignificant it may have been to them. One day at breakfast, my mother laughed at my father for mispronouncing "hors d'oeuvres." He did not appreciate being teased in front of my brother and me and told her to stop. I can't remember his exact words, but it was one of the few times he would not stand for her laughing at his expense. While I watched that interaction, the food I ate grew tasteless, like nothing more than sawdust. I will never forget that episode and how it reinforced my thoughts that arguing in front of young, impressionable children was not healthy or productive. (Of course, that's my belief. I know others may disagree.)

Yet, with my mother and grandmother deeply involved in such a somber profession, the weight of grief and sadness seemed inescapable. Maybe that's why they tried to avoid public arguments. We were surrounded by unending sadness with each funeral service. However, my parents didn't shy away from exposing my brother and me to the realities of their work at the funeral home. The family business was a shared responsibility, and I learned to understand the products and services being provided, even at a tender age. Answering phones before I could read or write became a natural part of my daily routine. Late-night calls and meetings with families in various neighborhoods taught me resilience and adaptability from an early age, shaping my personality in ways I couldn't have imagined.

Amidst our mostly harmonious family dynamic, several pivotal events shaped my life perspective and approach to challenges. At the age of thirteen, I had an eye-opening experience with birthday checks that I had saved over the years. Innocent and naïve, I approached my mother one day to cash those checks I'd stashed away, only to discover they were no longer valid. Not only that, but she also refused to rewrite the checks, so I never received those elusive birthday funds. Though disappointing, it was a valuable lesson in self-reliance and independence. From then on, I made sure to cash any checks immediately and ingrained this finance principle in my parenting style later in life.

As a young teenager, I already had ideas about where to go to school. My mother wanted me to attend an all-girls Catholic high school. That was the last thing I wanted. Half the world was made up of males! I wanted to interact with them, too. My father was teaching at the high school I wanted to attend. This was an urban, inner-city school with a great choir that I hoped to be a part of. I wanted to be among the choral students I had seen when I went to school programs with my father.

An experience at a summer camp when I was nine also influenced my desire to attend public school. I always loved the outdoors and wanted to go camping, so my parents sent me to a Catholic camp, although we were Baptists. My parents greatly respected the Catholic church, and my mother's stepfather was Catholic. At this camp, the kids had to get up early, walk to the outdoor chapel, and say their "Hail Marys."

I was the type of child who had to eat first before I walked that far so early in the morning. I informed the staff that I needed to have breakfast or I would faint. That fact made no difference to them. The policy was that you had to say "Hail Mary" on an empty stomach. Sure enough, I fainted each morning, and I was so afraid I was going to hit my head. That helped me decide that there was no way I would attend a Catholic school. I was scared to death!

My father, God bless him, said to my mother, "Vora (my mother's first name), if she does not want to go, don't make her." That simple but direct support saved me. At that time I attended the camp, I did not know how to handle a situation that might have been very dangerous for my health and well-being. Later, I made sure that my parenting style included informing my children what to do when they were in unsafe situations.

During my formative years at Sumner High School, I cherished some of the most remarkable moments of my life. Recognizing the significance of a good education and my passion for learning, I understood early on, around age twelve, the need to approach life seriously. Thanks to my father, who grasped the importance of my attending the school of my choice, I avoided a potentially miserable situation.

Just before high school began, he offered a unique incentive: five dollars for every "A" I achieved in my courses without lecturing me on the value of education or pressuring me to study diligently. Surprisingly, I was not as focused on the monetary rewards. From the start, I came home with straight "A's" on my first report card. My determination to excel was driven by the desire not to disappoint my father.

Attending Sumner filled me with joy and excitement, particularly in the classroom and the choir. I greatly respected my teachers and genuinely enjoyed studying, reading classic books, and completing my homework. After several rounds of high marks on my report card, my father stopped the financial rewards. I understood the message: he believed in my capabilities, which motivated me to strive for excellence more than finances ever could. Eventually, even my mother came to appreciate that Sumner was the right choice for me, further validating the importance of trusting my instincts.

My academic performance was outstanding as a high school senior, and I aimed to pursue higher education. However, an encounter with the principal proved challenging. He supported the male students and stated that they should receive priority treatment. He attempted to dissuade me from working so hard and pursuing my dreams. Resolute in my determination, I refused to be swayed and continued to excel. Eventually, I became the valedictorian of nearly 400 students, bringing immense pride to my family. This experience taught me the invaluable lesson of staying true to my chosen path, even in the face of discouragement from others.

Throughout my life, I have valued experiences, understanding people, obtaining an education, maintaining good health, and practicing my faith. Material possessions held little allure for me as I learned through my work in the funeral business how transient and insignificant possessions are in the grand scheme of life.

Cherishing memories of joyous childhood experiences, such as attending parties and singing in choirs, have provided me with more solace during difficult times in adulthood than possessions ever could. My high school years were among my happiest, thanks to my father's support and encouragement. These cherished memories became a source of strength during life's challenging times.

College Life

As a teenager, I eagerly anticipated the moment I could escape the confines of St. Louis and venture into the exciting world of higher education. I longed for the opportunity to break free from the rules and regulations my parents imposed on me, even though they weren't particularly strict. But as they say, that's just how teenagers are—seeking independence and asserting their individuality. Parents shouldn't take it personally; it's a natural part of growing up.

Independence was even more challenging for me because my family was quite well-known in the city because of the community funeral home and my father's work as a teacher. It often felt like I was under constant surveillance. No matter where I went, someone seemed to be watching me, and I couldn't get away with anything. My parents' friends were quick to report any missteps or unbecoming behavior, adding to the pressure to watch my every move.

Nonetheless, I consciously tried to observe and learn from my parents' actions. I vowed to remember what I would and wouldn't do when I had my children. My ultimate goal was to be independent and make my own decisions. I knew I could take care of myself, and college life provided the perfect opportunity to do so without my parents constantly watching and possibly disapproving of my choices.

Despite my desire for independence, I never wanted to disappoint my parents. Their love and approval meant the world to me. Going to college in another state seemed like the best option to explore my interests without fearing their disapproval.

The university I chose was partly influenced by my mother's enthusiastic praise for the institution. She had a remarkable time there, especially as a member of the esteemed Alpha Kappa Alpha Sorority. I had high expectations for a similar experience, but reality often has a way of surprising us.

Freshman year brought its own set of challenges, particularly because I was pledging to join my mother's sorority. Being away from home for the first time, I had to handle college courses, forge new connections, and maintain a balance all on my own. I resisted the urge to call my parents for advice, as I had been adamant about leaving home to prove my independence. With sheer determination and an unyielding spirit, I focused on my studies, ensuring I achieved the grade point average required for sorority induction.

The temptation to enjoy college life and engage in various distractions was ever-present, but I prioritized my studies first and foremost. When I rushed the sorority, pledging alongside seventeen others, only a fellow classmate named Retha and I made the cut, and we were inducted into the sorority in February of my second semester.

Amidst the challenges, I found encouragement and support from a student named Kenny, who remains a cherished friend to this day. I can vividly recall sitting under a tree on the quad, feeling distraught and overwhelmed by the overt racism I encountered almost daily at college. Coming from my diverse neighborhood in St. Louis, it was a foreign experience for me. Kenny's kind words and empathy were just what I needed to believe I could overcome those cruel and needless hurdles.

My love for learning remained unwavering, and I relished participating in class discussions, often seated at the front, eager to engage with my professors. Maybe some classmates saw me as "studying too much," but I didn't worry about that. My focus was on my education. With no job commitments during my freshman and sophomore years, I had ample time to delve into extracurricular activities, exploring diverse interests like fencing, ice skating, and music.

My academic journey wasn't without its share of traumatic events. One such incident occurred during my freshman year in a Physiology course. I had dedicated myself to diligent studying and nearly memorized the entire textbook. To my dismay, some teachers suspected me of cheating when I aced the final exam, leading to an unwarranted interrogation.

I took Rhetoric in my first semester and received an A from a professor. Another professor taught Rhetoric 2, and I was enrolled in his class. What surprised me was that I always received a C on all my assignments. I had never gotten a C, and certainly not in the first semester of Rhetoric class. I remember asking the teacher what was wrong with my assignments. My requests went unanswered. I was quite distraught and did not know what to do.

One day, this professor gave us an assignment to write about what historical period we would have liked to live in. I wrote my paper on wanting to live when Jesus Christ taught and preached. Unbeknownst to me, there was a policy of letting the Dean of the Department read the papers assigned to this class. The Dean came to my classroom and selected my paper as the best in the class. I stood up and was recognized for my work. I appreciated the acknowledgment, but how my professor treated me led me to believe there were other issues involved that I could not overcome. After that, I decided to transfer to another school where I hoped to encounter less bias and judgment. I still loved learning, but I was ready for a change.

With my parents' assistance, I transferred to a university on the East Coast, understanding that the credits I had already earned would be accepted. However, they unexpectedly reversed their decision upon arrival, demanding I repeat my sophomore year's classes. Fueled by my fighter instincts, I met with department chairs and presented a compelling case to be reinstated as a junior. It was astonishing how many obstacles I had to overcome compared to my peers. Still, my persistence prevailed, and I embraced my major in Psychology, a subject I had always been passionate about.

I dove headfirst into college life, living in a dorm across from my classes, meticulously planning my schedule to accommodate multiple jobs on afternoons and weekends. I also felt a responsibility to contribute financially to my education. From being a hospital switchboard operator to teaching English to a Spanish-speaking student and counseling at a youth community house, I engaged in various roles, valuing the opportunity to learn and grow. I also indulged in fencing, reading music, ice skating, and horseback riding classes, even overcoming a fall from my favorite horse, Ike, with unwavering determination.

After graduating, I chose a school on the West Coast of the United States to pursue my master's degree in social work. I was among many who observed a troubling pattern in the graduate program. The grading disparities between white students and students of color were evident, leading to a united demand for change. We fought for fairness and a more multicultural curriculum, determined to challenge the status quo.

Those experiences have shaped my character, instilling in me the courage to stand up for justice and equality. As I pursued my career and later became a parent, I imparted those valuable lessons to my children, ensuring they understood the importance of resilience and the fight for what is right. We certainly can't change the past, but we can fight for what is right and just.

Throughout my academic journey, I've learned that sometimes you don't know what you don't know, and when faced with challenges, it's essential to act beyond the norm and apply yourself fully. A setback doesn't have to be the end; instead, it's an opportunity to learn and grow stronger.

Today, I look back on my college years with a mix of fond memories, personal growth, and determination that has guided me throughout my life. It has been a remarkable journey, and I'm grateful for every obstacle and triumph that has shaped me into the person I am today.

My Career Path

After grad school, started my first full-time job at the Watts Health Center. I loved that job, and it was one of my happiest times. I remember interviewing for that job as a social worker in the mental health department. My soon-to-be boss asked me what I had learned in school. I answered by saying, "Absolutely nothing!" Then, I went on to explain my statement. Can you imagine being interviewed for a job and saying that you learned nothing in your school's graduate program? I still laugh at how naïve I was. I did not feel that the theories I had been taught prepared me for the clients that I was going to serve.

Fortunately, my boss understood the point I was trying to make. He probably appreciated my passion for learning what was pertinent for a job with the clients I knew I wanted to serve. I was outspoken and wanted to do the best I could.

Fortunately, he could see that desire in me and offered me the job. I learned so much from my three years at Watts. I also gave individual therapy to patients and learned a great deal from them. The problems my patients had and the toll it took on their lives taught me what not to do. Their difficulties taught me not to fall into those traps. My greatest satisfaction was helping them improve the quality of their lives. I have had much success in assisting people to better their lives.

I remember working with a Latina teenager who carried a Bible everywhere she went. She was referred to me for therapy. I discovered that teenagers can be challenging to work with and often don't want to talk too much.

I had finally made a treatment agreement with her to come and see me for therapy twice a week. After all that hard work of getting her to see me, I received a memo from the administration restricting all therapy sessions to once a week beginning immediately. This was so awkward for me since I was trying to have a breakthrough with my patient. All I could do was tell her the truth. Luckily, I could still help her despite the obstacles the administration had put in our path.

The patients that I treated had diagnoses ranging from anxiety to schizophrenia. Once I left the Watts Health Center, I reflected on the stories those brave people shared with me about their lives and what caused their problems and difficulties. I wanted to ensure that their issues and nonproductive behaviors were not repeated in their lives or in mine. I was learning, too. I owe most of my knowledge of how to relate to people from my social work training and the patients I had the honor and privilege to serve. In school, I was taught how to observe, listen, not pass judgment, and the importance of confidentiality. This has served me well throughout my career.

I had three great, diverse colleagues at Watts: one Caucasian, one Japanese, and one Mexican. We would call ourselves The International Four. We went out to lunch all the time, shared our life stories, and got along so well. The multicultural diversity was enlightening and refreshing. We learned how we were different and how we were alike. We accepted each other for who we were and who we wanted to be.

I never really recovered from that decision to restrict how often we saw our patients, and I decided that I needed to be in administration. I wanted to be part of the decision-making process. I needed to be able to make policy decisions that would enable employees to carry out their jobs successfully.

I applied to the University of Michigan's School of Public Health. I wanted to be a healthcare administrator. At that time, U of M had the number one program in Hospital Administration. I was lucky to get the stipend and scholarship I applied for. Without haste, I quit my California job, relocated to Ann Arbor, MI, and attended school full-time to get my second master's, this time in healthcare administration.

There, I met my first husband, Paul, who was a year ahead of me at U of M. He was brilliant and helped me study for my courses. It was a lot of fun, and we dated for a year. We were married after he graduated, and I was in my final year of school.

When I say the curriculum was demanding, I mean it was the most challenging of any school I had previously attended. We were required to have at least a B grade point average to graduate from the two-year program.

I can remember taking a course from one professor, but it was so traumatic that I blocked out the actual name of the class. I studied hard for the final exam. I knew how to study and was prepared for the test, or so I thought. I was sitting in the classroom waiting for the class to begin to take the final exam. The bell rang, and I opened the test booklet. I looked at the first question and could not even tell if the text was written in English! Terror consumed me. What would the other questions be like if this was the first one and it was this difficult?

I was able to rein in my high blood pressure and turn in the test, but I could not get over that first question. I was in bed at night going over and over it in my head. I finally figured out the answer. Early in the morning, I went to the professor's office and asked if I could answer that first question. I explained what had happened in class, with the panic attack, and how I had finally figured out what he was asking.

I reassured him that I had not cheated, asked anyone, or opened my notes or the textbook. That was the truth, and he believed me. He let me answer the question and gave me half credit. I was so relieved, not so much that I had gotten credit for the answer, but that I never gave up on trying to figure out what was being asked. Lesson learned: Always ask; you have nothing to lose—a lesson I always shared with my two girls.

After graduation from the University of Michigan, I eventually found employment where I could combine my mental health and hospital administration training. Quitting my job at the Watts Health Center and moving to Ann Arbor, MI, had not been easy. Saying goodbye to my California life and the friends I'd made was difficult, but I maintained contact with several of them as the years went by.

I always had fond memories of my years at the Watts Health Center in California. However, the most challenging part of my life was on the horizon—parenthood.

Family Life

As a young couple, Paul and I enjoyed our time together. We had great friends and would travel at will because we were all young and fancy-free. We would go to Glen Arbor, MI, and other vacation destinations. We went canoeing, played cards at each other's houses, and talked about all the fun we had in school. Most of us were in the same stage of life, recently graduated, and starting our professional careers. Those were the carefree days.

Three couples, including Paul and I, became pregnant in the same year, and we all gave birth to girls in 1979. Life changed for each of us as the children became our focus, and our group gatherings gradually decreased until they were practically nonexistent. Clearly, our lives were evolving, and we would have to go along with it. I did my best to focus on the positives, but I must admit that I missed those carefree days...and still do.

The First Child

Candice was eight pounds, three ounces at birth. I will never forget that initial loud cry; she had her tiny hands under her chin as if surveying her surroundings with piercing eyes. She was also in the upper percentile for weight. I had a glimpse of her personality right then and there, and I know other mothers who have felt the same way.

I knew my work would be cut out for me, and I was committed to giving her the best life possible. Yes, children can be molded by people and life's circumstances. However, they also bring their unique characteristics and personality traits. I have heard from mothers of multiples that they could tell babies were different in utero. Some babies may kick more than others, some may not like certain foods the expectant mother eats, and some are quiet.

The Second Child

Danielle was born three and a half years after Candice. She weighed almost nine pounds. She looked like a football player, I joked to myself. I could already tell by her temperament that she was different from Candice. She had a sweet cry and kept her eyes closed. Thank goodness I already had a plan in place because I used it to remind myself of that first year. It helped me maintain consistency in how I raised Candice. Here are a few things I learned with a second child.

Listening is increasingly important. When another sibling arrives, a parent has two children to acknowledge. Parents must try to listen to each child individually, which can be challenging. I can remember when they both could talk; there would be less than three seconds of silence before one of them started again. Children of any age need to feel that they are being heard. They need that attention. You are also teaching the child to listen to others as well. This is one way to build self-esteem.

It's also essential to let the child make age-appropriate decisions. I would ask Candice what she would like for dinner: broccoli or string beans. In that way, whatever the child decides is a good choice. I would give her options, but the ultimate decision was hers, and I was fine with either of them. Another example is when you have a child in a stroller, you can ask their opinion. *Do you want to take this sidewalk on the right or the one on the left?* Even if the child is too young to decide, they will begin to understand.

The more decisions you allow the child to make, the more they will learn. They will remember how you asked for their input. They also learn to think critically and analytically, which is immensely helpful in their development. They learn how to make daily decisions. Of course, the critical ones remained my responsibility.

Now that you know a bit about my family, let's take a deeper dive into the four parts of the PPP and how you can create one of your own.

Danielle, Candice, and me

4

Know Thy Self

The first step is to "know thy self," which means clearly understanding where you are in your life and what you want for yourself, personally and professionally. It's going to be a challenge to plan for your children if you haven't made your own plans first, the primary one being that you are prepared to accept the responsibility of being a parent.

When preparing to have children, it's essential to realize that life will change; it will be different. Life will have a new definition. Having children will be a life sentence but in a good way! Get ready to become another person, to some extent, another version of yourself. If you are realistic about the inevitable changes to your life, it will help you to acclimate. It is better not to focus on the changes that might be interpreted as unfavorable because there will be so many positive lifestyle changes that can result from having a family. Parenthood will usher in new life experiences that can be just as wonderful as your childless life, if not more so.

I was looking forward to having a baby, but I knew it would be challenging. Let me be completely honest: preparing for children is not easy. It requires you to re-examine everything that you know if you want to be successful. Having a psychology-based background can help inform your decision on the type of parent you hope to become.

Reading books on successful parenting (like this one!) can be helpful. With the endless opportunities that the internet allows, performing searches on topics like parenting and child development and any information you can get from reliable sources will help inform you.

That's exactly what I did. I found ways to educate myself because I firmly believe in being as prepared as possible. My parenting plan is the guide I developed to increase my chances of raising my children to the best of my abilities. Hopefully, some of the actions I took will be helpful to you as a parent.

When putting this guide together, I found all my notes and books on psychology, human behavior, and the latest theories of how best to raise a child. I thought about my children's challenges and how to prepare them for the best life possible. I was purposeful about considering the scenarios I experienced as a child and how I wanted to handle them as a parent.

The challenge was pulling all the information together because while I systematically approached parenting, I didn't write everything down. (I wish I had!) I used the teachings from college and my work experiences to build a plan that was right for me, and I went over it every night when I went to bed. I'd mentally review the day's events and how I responded, dissecting the events, thinking about my actions, and then deciding how I would tackle the next day. By doing that, my plan continued to form and eventually became a part of my everyday life. It wasn't a notebook on my nightstand; it was part of me. It was ingrained in my brain like a virtual notepad that I constantly referenced and updated with each new experience.

Of course, I realize not everyone is comfortable operating in that manner, so I encourage you to document your PPP as it develops and refer to it daily. Then it may become a part of you as well.

As a new parent, I considered what I liked and did not like about life, especially as a teenager. I vowed that I would make responsible parenting decisions. I was always thinking, remembering, and analyzing. I needed to incorporate all my life experiences, including knowledge I gained from classes and what I had learned from my patients and others I had interacted with. My grandmother said, "Plan for the worst and hope for the best." That became my mantra.

I knew I had to prepare my children to meet the challenges they would have in life. There was no way to avoid having difficulties. The key was to overcome them and not let them depress you or make you doubt your parenting skills. I got very little sleep during my first pregnancy because I was trying to figure out what kind of mother I needed to be to give my child the best start. It was a weighty responsibility. Failure was not an option.

I was determined to gather as much information and research as possible and synthesize it for what would work best for me. Knowing myself was critical in my choices and the plan I was developing. I decided very early that I had to start thinking about what type of mother I would be before the baby was born.

I had been thinking about having a family as a young teenager. For those who believe they will have children someday, it is never too early to start making wise decisions. As a young person, you can decide to be honest, hardworking, curious about life, not take drugs, get good grades, play team sports, etc. These experiences will be beneficial no matter what path you choose in life. The lessons that I learned in my family, on the job, with my friends and relatives, observing behaviors that I wanted to emulate, and deciding on behaviors I wanted to discard from my way of life had started very early.

I think most of us agree that education is the best investment a person can make to have a better life. Education includes what is learned directly and indirectly. Schooling teaches you how to analyze and learn how to think critically about theories the "experts" have. Don't believe everything you hear! As we get more and more data, beliefs change over the years. Yesterday's heresy is today's standard of care!

In my research, one of the now-debunked theories I read about in school is that a baby is like a blank slate. This is an example of a theory that was just incredibly inaccurate. Many researchers now believe that a baby's personality begins to form in the womb; thus, they are born with a predisposition.

That is why research shows that the mother's actions before birth may impact the baby. I believe there is truth to those theories. Future parents must consider how they want to conduct their lives before a child is born; the sooner, the better. Remember, it wasn't so long ago that women smoked and even drank alcohol during pregnancy if they wanted to because they didn't have the information that we have now.

Of course, I did what my obstetrician instructed me to do; I ate healthier than usual and tried not to do anything that would cause harm to my unborn baby. For instance, I loved banana splits and enjoyed them whenever possible. During the final weeks of the pregnancy, I remember going to Dairy Queen and having a huge banana split because I knew it would be my last. I was willing to sacrifice those ice cream treats in the future because they have no nutritional value and would not be good for my health. The real challenges would come after the baby was born and I needed to be healthy.

Here are some questions I considered that may help you:

- What sacrifices am I willing to make?
- Are there some things I am not willing to sacrifice?
- What type of life will I lead once the baby is born?
- Do I have the strength to do what is necessary to raise a child to be as healthy, happy, and well-adjusted as possible?

The journey of parenthood is undoubtedly filled with sacrifices, challenges, and difficult decisions. As you prepare to welcome a child, feeling excitement and apprehension is natural. But let me assure you, you can navigate this new chapter with grace and resilience, especially if you do a little planning ahead of time.

Parenthood is a transformative experience that will shape you in unexpected ways. Yes, there will be adjustments and sacrifices you hadn't anticipated, but remember that these changes can bring immense joy and fulfillment. Embrace the opportunity to grow and discover new depths of love and compassion within yourself.

It's essential to approach this journey with a positive mindset; instead of focusing on the things you might miss from your carefree days, shift your perspective to the incredible experiences that await you as a parent. Cherish the precious moments with your child, the laughter, the milestones, and the unconditional love that will fill your heart.

Preparing for parenthood means gathering knowledge and seeking guidance. Educate yourself about child development, parenting techniques, and strategies for nurturing a healthy and happy child. Take advantage of the online information but remember to trust your instincts and adapt the advice to suit your unique circumstances. There is no one-size-fits-all when it comes to parenting.

Remember, no one is perfect, and there will be moments of doubt and uncertainty. But trust in your ability to learn and grow alongside your child. Surround yourself with a support system of friends, family, and professionals who can offer guidance and reassurance when needed.

You are embarking on a remarkable journey that will test your patience, resilience, and unconditional love. Embrace the challenges, celebrate the victories, and remember you are not alone. You have what it takes to be a fantastic parent, and your child will be forever grateful for the love and care you provide.

Creating your personalized plan is crucial in establishing a harmonious and nurturing environment for your family. It's a dynamic process that evolves as your family grows and changes. We will explore various ways to organize and structure your parenting plan, allowing you to tailor it to your unique family needs and preferences.

When you begin crafting your plan, it's essential to start by gathering all the relevant information. You may have already collected valuable insights during your self-assessment and research phases. Now, it's time to organize this wealth of data effectively.

First, don't worry too much about the format or topics; jot down your ideas and see what you get. You can always go back and finesse them if you like. Here are mine:

- I am a fighter.
- I will never give up.
- I am a hard worker.
- I observe and listen to other people.
- I am more objective than emotional.
- I plan for the worst and hope for the best.
- I try to avoid making the mistakes that other people make.
- I am a planner.
- I want to incorporate all that I am into a plan for raising children.

Format for Success

Once you have your basic topics, it's time to fine-tune your ideas by choosing a format for your parenting plan. Remember, there's no one-size-fits-all approach; it should be something that resonates with you and fits your lifestyle. Here are some options to consider.

Journal: A journal is excellent for those who enjoy a more informal and narrative approach. You can record your thoughts, experiences, and observations as your parenting journey unfolds. It's a way to capture the emotional aspects of parenting along with practical details.

Notepad with Sections: If you prefer more structure, consider using a notepad with individual sections. Each section can focus on different aspects of your parenting plan, making finding and updating specific information easier.

Folder with loose pages: A folder with pages is a versatile choice for flexibility and longevity. You can add, remove, or rearrange pages as needed. This format is handy if you anticipate your plan evolving over time.

Tablet or smartphone: Many applications for taking notes can be useful for someone who uses their phone or tablet a lot and wants to jot things down quickly. Later, you can go back and clarify or organize your thoughts. You can also add alerts to remind you when it's time to update or review your plan.

Some people find that there is something therapeutic about actually writing things down by hand. They find that the tactile experience somehow makes it more personal. It's also a way to escape having to type on a keyboard, especially if you do that every day at work. Handwriting might help you to internalize your plan without reminding you of your job. The point is to choose what is best for you and your situation, with the ultimate goal of committing your PPP to memory like I did. It should become so ingrained in your daily activities that you will gradually become less dependent on the written word and more attuned to your own instincts. If you can embody the plan, it will become more organic and thus more impactful.

Get Organized

Once you've chosen your format, it's time to decide on your organizational style. Your style can be as casual or as detailed as you like. Some prefer to write things out in complete sentences, while others like using to-do lists. Here are examples of contrasting approaches.

Casual Style with Bulleted Lists: If you prefer a more relaxed and straightforward approach, create a parenting plan using bulleted lists. You can jot down key points, ideas, and goals in a simple, easy-to-read format. This style is great for busy parents who want to keep things concise. Something like this:

- Morning routine
- Breakfast together

- School drop-off
- Playtime
- Evening routine
- Homework
- Dinner as a family
- Bedtime story

Detailed Style with Headings and Objectives: For those who appreciate structure and thorough planning, use headings, objectives, goals, outlines, and even references to parenting resources. This style allows for comprehensive planning and a deep understanding of your parenting approach.

Whatever method you choose, remember that you can always switch gears if it's not working for you. Try one way and then another until you find a comfortable approach that fits your lifestyle.

A Balanced Plan

If you're not sure how to begin, begin with a basic scenario. Create a realistic routine that fosters both academic growth and quality family time. Start with the age-appropriate basics; you can go back and fill in more details as you think of them.

Morning routine:

7:00 AM - 7:30 AM: Breakfast as a family
7:30 AM - 8:00 AM: School drop-off
8:30 AM - 3:00 PM: School hours
3:30 PM - 4:30 PM: Homework and study time
4:30 PM - 6:00 PM: Free play or structured extracurricular activities

Evening routine:

6:30 PM - 7:30 PM: Dinner as a family

7:30 PM - 8:00 PM: Bath time and bedtime preparations
8:00 PM - 8:30 PM: Bedtime story and cuddle time
8:30 PM: Lights out!

The Personal Touch

To make your parenting plan more meaningful, consider adding personal touches. You can include references to your favorite parenting books or inspirational quotes that resonate with your values and beliefs. These elements can serve as reminders of your guiding principles as parents.

As you embark on this journey of creating your PPP, remember that it's a living document. It should reflect your family's unique dynamics and adapt as your children grow and your circumstances change. Make it enjoyable to reference, and keep it updated to ensure it remains a valuable resource for your family's evolving needs.

Danielle, me, and Candice in Ireland

5

Develop the Plan

Step two of the process is developing the plan to become your PPP. That means applying the decisions you've made, like how you will start to document your plan and begin pulling it together using the suggestions in this chapter.

Preparation

As a healthcare administrator, I often made strategic plans for our healthcare systems. I understood the importance of having a vision of setting goals and objectives to succeed. A mission statement and tasks must be carried out to accomplish identified tasks.

Now that you understand who you are and what you want for your child, you can create a PPP that reflects your strengths, weaknesses, opportunities, and threats (SWOT). So, there is no confusion, let's level-set by agreeing on these definitions:

- Strengths: Characteristics that provide an advantage.
- Weaknesses: Characteristics that create a disadvantage relative to others.
- Opportunities: External chances for improvement.

- Threats: External elements that could cause disruption or trouble.

Identifying scenario options to address what you now know about yourself is vital to developing a successful PPP. In other words, what scenarios do you need to imagine ensuring that the PPP can be implemented successfully? You want to have several different approaches to dealing with adversity. This is why knowing oneself is essential to success in parenting and life.

By the time I finished college, I had a solid understanding of who I was. I knew my strengths and weaknesses. I had to remember not to judge whether one of my character traits was bad or good. I just needed to recognize it and work with it.

The point is that we don't have to take our circumstances at face value and assume there are no other options and choices. We can use that knowledge to our benefit, make the best of our hand, and realize that no one always has a winning hand.

This is where preparation comes into play, and I truly believe God helps those who help themselves. Some idioms that I find inspiring include:

- Prevention is worth a pound of cure.
- You put in the time now or pay a hefty price later.
- Plan for the worst and hope for the best.

The purpose of my plan was to not only help with parenting but also to guide me through my life. Having established goals would keep me on solid ground to meet my parenting and personal objectives. Many of my lessons came from what my parents said and did. I also learned from them what I did not want to do as a parent and included those in my PPP.

Here are some tips when creating your own plan:

1. *Identify your strengths.* Develop your PPP by focusing on your strengths. For example, if you have a job requiring knowledge and skills that are similar to those used when raising children, that is a strength. Leverage those attributes as you design your PPP. Research the internet or your local library for information on parenting, psychology, and childhood development from trustworthy sources and identify areas where you have experience. Put all this information together to identify your strengths.
2. *Accept your weaknesses.* We all have weaknesses! No one is perfect. Knowing your weaknesses will not only help your plan but will also positively impact your life in general. Knowledge is power, and self-knowledge is the most powerful of all. Use your weaknesses to design a PPP that compensates for those areas. Identify people who can complement you to be part of your village. Allow them to help fill in those areas where you may need assistance. Knowing how to compensate for weaknesses strengthens us and improves our parenting skills. Allow your friends and family to assist when needed because we can all use help occasionally.
3. *Explore opportunities.* This may take some thought, but there are opportunities that you may need to identify. For example, you may have friends or colleagues with a wealth of information you can tap into. Your community may have classes that you can take that will provide you with information that can be helpful. Some people take classes and never apply the knowledge they gained to their lives, so be mindful of how to use what you learn. There is often a way to practically apply any new information to your life; the PPP can help you visualize that.
4. *Mitigate threats.* How are you going to be able to recognize and overcome obstacles? Some of the threats will not be apparent at first, and even if they are, you may be unable to control them. First, you will need to learn how to identify the hazards. Be

aware of roadblocks or obstacles that slow you down. Pay attention to what is happening around you. Once a threat is identified, determine how to avoid or mitigate it. Some examples of common threats include illness, financial difficulties, environmental conditions, cultural differences, etc. Just be aware and take appropriate steps to better protect your child and yourself.

If you have gotten as far as knowing yourself, you have done the most critical work to start building your PPP. There are probably bits and pieces of the PPP that you already know must be included. Now, you need to organize it and complete the first draft.

The first step is to get started. Be as brief or detailed as you want, but get something down to start building your plan. The goal is to continue adding to it as you learn and grow as a parent. You can even identify goals you want to accomplish in the future, like getting the baby to sleep through the night.

Sometimes, it will be necessary to revise the PPP, and that's fine. It is meant to be a document that grows with you. It should be adjusted as your life circumstances change. I constantly evaluated my plan to ensure it represented what needed to be done at a particular point in my life. I would lie in bed at night and review my mental checklist for areas of improvement. I would recreate the scenarios and wonder if I could have handled a situation differently. I was focused on using my new parenting experiences as learning opportunities.

I thought about the parenting styles of my parents and grandmother and how that impacted me and my brother. Their intentions were genuine, and most of the way they raised us was helpful and prepared us for life's challenges. I knew I had been loved, which is probably the most important, but they certainly weren't without fault.

Each generation should analyze how they were raised and determine what to continue and what to avoid. Returning to corporate jargon, it's the Start, Stop, Continue method. Start good parenting practices, stop those you feel do not work, and continue the ones you want to incorporate into your parenting style. In that way, each generation benefits from evolved parenting styles.

Development

Identify your mission and your vision. The mission will likely be straightforward, such as "ensure the baby is healthy." Your vision might be a far-off goal, for example, "to see my children graduate from college and get a good job."

For me, the mission was the foundation of my plan. My ultimate mission was to ensure my baby was alive and healthy. I knew that I had to be careful in making risky personal decisions. My primary consideration was keeping my child out of harm's way. This is an extreme example, but I remember seeing on the news a parent placing a child close to a bear to take a picture! That was something I would never do.

But on the other hand, you must learn when to leave well enough alone. I had to remind myself that if a relative or friend was saying or doing things to my child that I did not like, I just let it go if it was not harmful or life-threatening. I advise new parents to listen politely to the suggestions of family and friends. It doesn't hurt to hear them out and think about their point of view. You do not have to get into arguments and nonproductive debates about how you are raising your children.

Be careful to select the people supporting your parenting goals to be with your children when you are unavailable. Here are some rules I learned early in my parenting journey that applied as a new parent and as the children got older:

1. *The baby comes first.* I decided I would not get involved in anything that took too much time away from the baby. I also chose not to do anything that might cause me harm. For example, I decided to discontinue high-risk activities, like my favorite

sport – horseback riding, which is often ranked as one of the most dangerous sports. I was no longer willing to risk possible injury with a child to raise. Eventually, I stopped playing tennis because I was very competitive and unwilling to play enough tennis to continue improving. Even though the baby was my priority, I recognized that I had to ensure that I was healthy to care for her. I had to come first so I could then put them first! This was the paradox! It will be necessary for you to get as much rest, support, and whatever you need as a human being to be a thoughtful, purposeful parent so you can be properly guided by the PPP.

2. *Provide structure and consistency.* If my baby started crying, I had to get up, whether I was tired or sick. I had to develop a routine so she could have some expectation that I would be there for her. As parents, that's a sacrifice we have to make. When she was in daycare, I was always concerned about her welfare. There was routine and structure, and I had to tell myself they knew more about caring for children than a first-time mother.

As Candice got older, I paid attention to her demeanor as I dropped her off and picked her up from daycare. She never showed any fear or unhappiness. A young child cannot tell you if they are being treated well, so you must look for signs. I had no other choice since I had to go to work every day. That meant finding quality care was crucial for my stress level and peace of mind so that I could focus on my work.

For quality childcare, the best thing a parent can do is ask other parents for their recommendations. Look at the licensing requirements, quality of staff, staff-to-child ratio, and facility conditions. Also, do not hesitate to drop by unannounced and stay alert to continue monitoring the childcare setting. Do your best to select the childcare facility that will work for you and your child. There was no working from home when my children were small, but thankfully, there are more remote working opportunities today, and that can reduce the need for full-time childcare. I tried never to underestimate how much an infant experiences. I assumed that no matter what age, an infant is aware of their surroundings and the care they receive. So, I was extremely careful of where I left my children, keeping in mind both the people and the environment.

3. *Stay mindful to manage your stress level.* I worked hard not to take my frustrations out on my children. Negative emotional outbursts would be counterproductive. I had watched parents yelling at the top of their voices, "Stop that!" "Don't do that!" "Shut up!" "If I told you once, I have told you a thousand times," etc. Children often acclimate to that approach, and it can influence their behavior in the long term. The only effect was probably to raise the blood pressure level of the parent doing the screaming. I tried to remain aware of my mood and demeanor. I disciplined myself to speak softly, even if I wanted to scream because that's a natural reaction. The children learned that the more soothing my voice, the angrier I was. It was challenging to maintain that control, but I felt it was necessary. As parents, it's up to us to set the tone and manage our emotional outbursts around our children. It does get easier as the years go by!

4. *Be careful of the language you use.* I consciously tried to ensure that no cursing or foul language was spoken in my home. That decision would prevent me from slipping and saying an inappropriate word or making a controversial statement in the wrong setting. I made that decision because I did not want my children to think using that language was appropriate. I have heard other children innocently say words or statements that embarrassed their parents, and I wanted to curtail that. Of course, they would be exposed to unsavory language at some point, but setting expectations at home was important to me.

5. *Reinforce the behavior you want your child to repeat.* One lesson I learned in my psychology classes is that positive reinforcement is more effective than punishment. This ties into the careful use of language. I was diligent about reinforcing what I considered good behavior. If my baby smiled, she would get kisses, hugs, and complimentary statements from me. Candice was a loud crier. Even after being fed, bathed, and diapered, she would cry loudly. I would always check to ensure everything was okay. Soon, she figured out that loud crying was not effective. I was more attentive and affectionate when she was not screaming. Parents can reinforce behaviors they want to encourage, but I found that all behaviors are important in some way. Unacceptable behavior should be identified and corrected so the child will be able to differentiate that from behavior that is encouraged and reinforced (which is not the same as rewarded).

6. *Communication and listening are essential.* These are some of the most critical parts of the PPP. As parents, you must learn and master how to communicate and listen. Speaking effectively was my goal. When children are young, it's often necessary to be direct. I knew in my social work training that listening is so critical. Listening means that you clear your mind and refrain from judgment. Looking them in the eye when they speak and listening to what they *do not* say can make all the difference. I would make plenty of eye contact with my children when I talked to them to ensure effective communication and listening. I always tried to let them know how important they were to me. I refrained from using "baby talk." When they made babbling sounds, I told them I heard them and would always look them in the eye. This took a lot of effort on my part. Candice babbled all day, and I responded as much as I could. I remember one day, I was dressing her when she was less than one year old. She gazed into my eyes, and I returned her gaze. I felt an undeniable connection as I looked into her eyes and tried to communicate

how much I loved her. I always wondered what effect the gazing had on her, but I knew that it was meaningful to me.

7. *Model acceptable behavior consistently.* That means you must show them how you expect them to act daily. It would be best to always handle situations in a way that teaches them how to handle life's problems. I tried to always be respectful to others; I would not be judgmental when people had different beliefs; I would try to understand why people do what they do; and I would handle adverse situations calmly and thoughtfully. A parent should spend time with children and teach them the values and behaviors that will help that child grow into an adult you can be proud of. That doesn't mean it comes easily, but if you remain "purposeful" in your approach, the rest will fall into place.

8. *Focus on how they feel about themselves.* It is essential to nurture your child's self-esteem. Understanding their thoughts is a priority; parents must take this seriously. Are they shy? Can they handle criticism? Are they having trouble at school that they are embarrassed about? Do they take ordinary problems too seriously? I tried to ensure my children understood that there was much more to them than their physical appearance. What was important was how they thought about themselves. My goal was to help them become strong, self-confident, happy, expressive people who would be comfortable in all settings. I shared with them that they are descendants of kings and queens from Egypt, one of the oldest civilizations in the world. I wanted them to learn to be confident about who they were, not just how they looked.

9. *Delegate to others.* I knew I had specific weaknesses and needed more skill in some areas. For instance, if I wanted to homeschool my children, that would not have been an option. I had an outside job, and I was not a trained teacher. Private schools were too expensive for me to consider. Instead, I sent my children to an excellent public school system. Another weakness I

had was sex education. I knew I would be too subjective to instruct my girls in this area. I delegated this responsibility to my ex-husband's wife, Michelle, who was like a second mother to my girls. Michelle is a nurse, and I knew she would do a better job than I could. I was relieved to have this option! Delegating specific child-raising activities to someone who might do a better job than you can is a blessing! It manages your weaknesses and reduces stress.

10. *Leave work stress at work.* As you drive home or take public transportation, tell yourself that you will not bring those bad feelings from your job to your home. Leave it at the doorstep. When you see your children, it's a joyous time, and you should remember to take full advantage of it. Don't let work issues interfere. Shift your focus to them. Ask how their day was! Work will still be there tomorrow.

11. *Try not to get frustrated.* There will be times when you don't know what to do. No matter how much you prepare, plan, think, or agonize over situations, there may not be an obvious answer. This is when you must make a judgment call. During stressful situations, you can only do your best. Remember to have confidence in yourself when making these decisions because of all the previous work of knowing yourself. You will have learned you are capable. You will know where your strengths are. This will be the time to refer to the PPP as a reminder. That's what it's for!

Candice and Danielle, around ages 6 and 2

6

Execute the Plan

The third step in the PPP development process is to execute your plan. Before you begin, you should know several things to help you successfully implement the PPP you have worked hard to develop. Prevention is the fundamental goal, so you want to take it seriously. I am sure you have heard the saying, "A stitch in time saves nine." There is so much truth in that. Take it to heart!

The following information will help prepare you for implementing the PPP. Putting in this pre-work will pay off in the end.

Be Aware of Defensiveness

People use defense mechanisms such as sublimation (unacceptable feelings are channeled into positive, socially acceptable behaviors) and anticipation (planning for the future to address life's challenges) to manage undesirable feelings and thoughts. These defense mechanisms tend to be valuable ways of handling difficulties in life.

Parents should be aware that some defense mechanisms can unintentionally affect their parenting. I'll be highlighting those that are often the most challenging. From my psychology studies, I've learned about various actions like projection, denial, displacement, and rationalization. These were first identified by Sigmund Freud as unconscious strategies we use to shield ourselves from anxiety, fear, and threats to our self-esteem or to avoid behaviors we deem unacceptable. Understanding these can greatly enhance parenting skills.

- <u>Projection</u> - This refers to projecting your own challenging thoughts and feelings onto someone else. For instance, you might mistakenly think your child has negative traits when, in reality, these are behaviors or attitudes you possess. It's important to be cautious and not mistakenly ascribe your own difficulties to your child.
- <u>Denial</u> – This involves refusing to acknowledge reality. This happens when you encounter situations that are too difficult to confront, leading you to ignore or block out what's actually happening. It's widely recognized as a potentially harmful defense mechanism, and I concur. Embracing honesty and facing facts is crucial. It's important to see and accept reality as it is, rather than denying it, to ensure that you're setting a positive example for your child. Children observe and learn from everything you do and say, so teaching them to understand and accept reality is essential.
- <u>Displacement</u> – This is a defense mechanism I learned about in psychology class, where aggression toward a more powerful individual is redirected toward someone or something less threatening. For example, if you've had a rough day at work and couldn't express your frustrations to your boss, you might come home and take out your anger inappropriately, like being short-tempered with your pet. This is known as "kicking the dog" syndrome. It's crucial to avoid using your children as outlets for frustrations that stem from other areas of your life.
- <u>Rationalization</u> – This involves creating excuses for your children's behavior, often ignoring the actual facts. While it's natural to want to protect your kids, it's also important to hold them accountable for their actions. Failing to correct them

when necessary or allowing them to persist in behaviors that won't contribute to their success is not beneficial for their development. Encouraging responsibility and understanding is key to their growth.

Avoid Unacceptable Behavior

We all have our imperfections, being human. There are certain behaviors, however, that we can manage more effectively. I recall watching a TV show where mothers and daughters were interviewed. One question posed to an adult daughter was about what her mother does that annoys her. She mentioned that her mother often talks during movies, something she finds irritating. She even joked that her mother would be the one in the movie theater causing a disturbance with her constant talking.

When the mother's friends were asked about this, the mother admitted to talking through films. Surprisingly, she revealed that she does it intentionally to annoy her daughter. This behavior struck me as a bit mean-spirited. Intentionally irritating your children isn't advisable. Such actions are within our control, and choosing a more positive approach can lead to a better relationship.

Minimize Guilt and Regret

First, let's define the two so that we have the same understanding.

- Guilt is the sensation of remorse or responsibility one experiences after doing something they perceive as wrong or harmful, whether it's actual or just perceived. It can manifest as a sense of worry or unhappiness. For instance, a person might feel guilty for leaving their children alone or not spending enough time with their children. Importantly, guilt can also act as a helpful indicator, guiding us to recognize the impact of our actions

on ourselves and others and encouraging personal growth and mindfulness in our behavior.
- Regret is the emotion of sadness or disappointment that arises from events or actions, either things you did or didn't do. For instance, you might regret a decision to leave school early or a mistake you've made. Additionally, regret is often expressed formally, especially in writing, to convey sorrow about disappointing or unpleasant situations. For example, you might say, "I regret that you did not gain admission to Harvard," to express sympathetic disappointment for someone's missed opportunity. Regret can also encourage reflection and learning from past experiences, leading to better choices in the future.

The goal of your parenting plan is to reduce the likelihood of making decisions that you might later feel guilty or regretful about. Imagine if you could remove the burden of guilt and regret from your thoughts. As much as possible try to steer clear of dwelling on these feelings as much as possible, as they can negatively impact your mental health, especially when following your PPP.

It's common for parents to experience guilt or regret; these emotions are natural, particularly when we deeply care for our children. Yet, with effort, you can learn to lessen the impact of these unhelpful and self-critical feelings. Dwelling on past mistakes or missed opportunities is not a productive use of time and energy. Remember, you always make the best decisions you can based on your knowledge and experiences at the time. It's important to forgive yourself and acknowledge that being human involves making mistakes and learning from them.

Let Your Children Decide Their Future

Some parents have preconceived ideas about what their children should do with their lives, whether it is a profession, a place to live, the type of education, or ultimately how they should live their lives. There may have been circumstances that did not permit the parents to realize their dreams, so they project that onto their children. They want to live out their dreams vicariously.

The children may be perfectly aligned with those dreams and goals. However, in most cases, children have talents and interests that take them in another direction. They need to be supported in what they want to do.

There is nothing wrong with sitting your children down and ensuring they understand that their future is up to them and you are there to support their dreams as much as possible. Remember to avoid making them feel guilty or stressed out because they have ideas for their future. After all, it's their life to live.

Follow the Plan

The most important part of your Positive Parenting Program (PPP) is having a well-thought-out plan in place designed to navigate the challenges of parenting effectively. To make this easier, consider following these three steps for each situation you face:

1. Identify – Recognize and acknowledge the activity that you are concerned about.
2. Commit – Make a conscious decision to ensure that every encounter involving this type of activity is as safe as possible.
3. Implement – Come up with creative and innovative ways to create a safe environment.

A key element of any parenting plan is ensuring the safety and well-being of your child, which varies with their age and needs. For example, infants require constant care and supervision, whereas school-age children might need less. It's important to tailor your plan to both your and your child's specific situation.

I find that real-life examples clarify concepts best. Let me share how I used the method "identify, commit, implement" in our morning routine. Recognizing the importance of a structured morning, I taught my young daughters to call for me when they woke up so they wouldn't get up before I was ready. I committed to this approach firmly. Upon hearing them, I'd go to their room, greet them, and help them start their day. This method worked well, but it meant they woke up at 6 a.m. daily, requiring me to rise early, too. It was challenging but necessary for their safety, especially since they could climb out of their cribs by their second year.

The implementation of my plan varied with each child. One required less involvement, while the other needed more hands-on attention because she was younger. The crucial point was my willingness to adapt my approach to suit each child's personality and needs. We must be ready to adjust our plans to meet the unique challenges each child presents.

The takeaway is the importance of identifying key areas in your parenting and applying these principles to develop a personalized PPP that works for you and your children.

Review Your PPP

The PPP should be reviewed periodically to ensure it aligns with your goals. I thought about my plan so much that it was engraved in my brain. It was seared into my DNA. I knew that I had to make sure I could carry it out. There are many ways to get off track, give up, and resort to habits you may have had before the children were born that are not good for raising a happy, healthy child. I needed to muster the necessary strength every day to follow my plan.

To do that, I had to develop a philosophy that prevented me from getting discouraged. I convinced myself to look at life as if all things are possible. Even when adverse events happened, my mindset was that everything would be alright. Rain or shine, sickness or health, financial challenges, bad days on the job, I had to keep an even keel. As hard as this was when I was younger, and my children were small, I learned this approach worked well for me. As the years went by, it got easier and came more naturally. Following my PPP became second nature; it became part of my routine, like brushing my teeth. Knowing it is always there for reference, encouragement, and strength made me feel better about my decisions.

Building a solid mindset means reminding yourself that things are going well or will soon improve, especially with a healthy outlook. It sounds like brainwashing, but it's a form of positive thinking. If you think good things will come, they will likely follow suit.

Another technique I used almost daily was "pressing the automatic button in my brain." It was too difficult and depressing to think about everything I had to do each day and the fact that I did not have enough time to complete all the tasks that needed to be accomplished, so I had to become very organized and efficient. This is when I became what I call a robot. That means I was completely focused as if I had blinders on. I didn't allow other issues to derail or distract me.

The alarm would clang in the morning, and I was off! I'd wake the kids, get them dressed, feed them breakfast, make sure they caught the school bus, get myself ready, and drive through rush-hour traffic to reach the office. Usually, I'd have a busy day and hope for no distractions, like calls from the school or the babysitter not being available. Those situations sometimes happened, but I knew I had to manage them with objective, well-thought-out responses.

I would drive home, expect the babysitter to feed the girls and supervise their music practice, somehow eat dinner myself, go over their homework, and get them in bed by 8 p.m. I would be exhausted, but I still had other work to do, either housework or office work. This was my routine Monday-Friday, day after day, week after week, month after month, year after year.

The weekends were filled with activities for the children, where I donned my chauffeur hat. Going to track meets and other extracurricular events kept me busy. In between, I had to go grocery shopping, do some house cleaning, spend quality time with my daughters, and ensure we were prepared for the next week. Often, I had job-related duties that I had to complete as well. Sometimes, I would be paged and had to address a work issue.

While taking time for yourself is essential, it can be challenging. Once, I had a free Sunday afternoon, and it was like a slice of heaven. However, I wasn't sure what to do with myself. The children were at an activity and being supervised, so I didn't have to worry about that. Finally, I decided to take in a movie matinee. I had not seen a film in a theater since the girls were born. It was a true luxury.

While in the theater, I received a notice on my pager: "The hospital is on fire!" I jumped up and ran to my car. I drove faster than I have ever driven in my life. The only thing going more quickly was my heartbeat. I did not know what to expect or how I might react.

When I arrived at the hospital, the fire had been extinguished. A patient with a head injury had been smoking and accidentally dropped the lighted cigarette. The wonderful nurses had acted quickly. By the time I got there, there was plenty of smoke still in the air, and the patients had been evacuated, but the situation was handled. Even the family members had been notified. God bless the nurses! I cannot tell you how much I appreciate them. They made my job so much easier. However, it was a long time before I could relax enough to go to another movie matinee.

I could have been upset about the hospital fire interrupting my rare movie visit, but I didn't see it that way. It was fortuitous that the children were cared for by a previously scheduled activity, and I was able to get to the hospital at record speed. The nurses were so competent when I arrived; most of what needed to be done had already been accomplished. I was glad that things turned out well and everyone was safe. Movies would come and go. It was all about my perspective.

That moment reminded me to stick to the plan no matter what curveball life might throw my way. I knew what I was doing now would enable me to reap the benefits later in life. Part of my plan was to put in the necessary time and energy early in my children's lives so that the later years would show the benefits.

Remember, the aim is for your PPP to seamlessly integrate into your daily routine, eventually becoming a natural part of your lifestyle. Critical moments like a child reaching a new milestone or the birth of a sibling present ideal opportunities to revisit and, if necessary, revise the PPP. The plan must evolve in tandem with the growth and development of your children.

As I embarked on my second year of parenting, it became evident that I needed to update my plan to cater to the emerging needs of a toddler. Each new stage in a child's life requires parents to adapt and modify their approach. In the initial year, a parent makes all decisions for the child, ensuring their safety in a crib or playpen and determining their schedule for bathing, eating, and playing. However, significant revisions to my plan were necessary when my first daughter turned two, and I welcomed my second child into the world. These changes were vital to address a growing family's shifting dynamics and needs.

Make Plan Consistent

Think about what strengthens you as a person and parent. My early days in the church were so helpful in giving me the strength to endure the immense amount of effort required to implement my parenting plan. God helps those who help themselves. It seems like this proverb originated in ancient Greece, but regardless, prayer was essential because I needed all the help I could get. When I prayed, I asked God to give me the strength to overcome adversity. I knew that life would have its ups and downs. I tried to be realistic when I asked God for help.

"Pain is inevitable; suffering is optional," said the Japanese writer Haruki Murakami. I wanted God to give me the strength to raise my two girls and live long enough to see them become adults. I asked that my parenting be successful and that I do my best to make them well-adjusted human beings.

When times were tough, I would think about my favorite poem, "Footprints in the Sand" by Mary Stephenson. It tells of a person walking in the sand, talking to the Lord with two pairs of footprints. Only one set of prints existed when the person walking had the most difficult times. The person asked the Lord where he was when he needed him the most. God replied, "That is when I carried you."

The years before both of my daughters went away to college were the most challenging and stressful of my entire life. I told myself the teenage years are so tricky because nature makes it easier for you to be glad the teenagers are leaving home, either to go to college or go out on their own. I had a plan, but it wasn't easy to implement it every day. I was exhausted and anxious, wondering if I could be successful while managing comments and even criticism from friends and relatives about how I was raising my two girls.

I did several things to fortify myself for the responsibility that was before me. I knew I needed to prepare myself in case I had a meltdown or had to make a judgment call regarding the girls. There were so many of those situations.

Right after Danielle was born, I used to lie awake worrying about everything that could go wrong. I was the type of person who wanted to know what to do if faced with a challenging situation. I did not want to be caught by surprise and unable to make a good decision, especially if the decision involved my children. I knew that I had to put my emotions on the back burner. Allowing myself to be emotional would not help me make sound choices. Many a night, I thought about the most horrible situations I might face and how I would deal with them if they occurred.

I planned for the worst and hoped for the best since I had learned that people who plan for adverse situations seem better prepared to handle them. Some of the problems that I tried to solve preemptively were clearly rare occurrences like what if the children needed an organ transplant; what if they were kidnapped; what if they were in an accident and ended up in the hospital; what if my plan was not working; what if I lost my job; what if I lost my life. What if… what if… what if.

My plan included some of my favorite poems, sayings, movies, and songs to help keep me centered. Sometimes, especially during challenging times, I would think about a poem or song or poem, and it would help remind me to stay on course. I encourage you to do the same.

Two of my favorite poems:

- "If" by Rudyard Kipling
- "Footprints in the Sand" by Mary Stevenson

Favorite sayings:

- Plan for the worst and hope for the best.
- Spend some and save some for a rainy day.
- I was born with a handful of cards: some winning cards, some losing cards, and some cards that could go either way.

Favorite Movies:

- *Goodbye Mr. Chips* (1939)
- *Song of Bernadette* (1943)

Favorite songs:

- "Rescue Me" by Fontella Bass
- "Say a Little Prayer" by Aretha Franklin

In the next chapter, I vividly recount various notable experiences I faced while executing my parenting plan for raising my daughters. These events are organized alphabetically and thematically for ease of access and reference. Each situation is followed by the solution I applied and my thought process behind these decisions.

Self-reflection is a pivotal aspect of personal and parental development. I consistently learned from my actions and those of my daughters, applying these insights to future situations. I viewed these experiences as opportunities for all of us to grow. Embracing the necessity of learning and evolving is essential, and I believe we largely succeeded in this endeavor.

I hope you have a similar experience with your lessons in parenting.

Danielle is dressed for one of her dance recitals

7

Lessons in Parenting

Here, you will find a list of topics I addressed in my parenting journey. Some of these situations focus on the child, some on the parent, and some on both. Hopefully, these will give you some ideas for your plan. You will see the examples organized by situation, solution, and rationale to help preview how this information is organized.

Accountability

Children inherently need and thrive on structure and consistency in their lives. They must feel that they can depend on the stability of their daily routine and trust that promises made to them are kept. For example, if you advocate against consuming alcoholic beverages for health reasons, it's imperative to refrain from drinking in front of your children. Likewise, if you value the importance of a good night's sleep, ensure your children adhere to a reasonable bedtime, setting an example by doing the same yourself. Similarly, enforcing regular school attendance is essential if education is a priority, barring extraordinary circumstances.

Regarding parental aspirations, it's common for parents to envision their children fulfilling the dreams they could not achieve.

However, it's essential to recognize and embrace each child's unique interests and talents, even if they diverge from the parent's unfulfilled ambitions. Supporting children in their chosen paths is critical, but they must understand that they are accountable for their choices and actions. Engaging them in honest discussions about their goals and the dedication required to achieve them is beneficial and necessary. This approach fosters an environment of understanding and encouragement, guiding children to realize their potential and dreams.

Situation: Candice was in her senior year of high school. She applied to college and was accepted early after she graduated. Apparently, after being accepted, she stopped attending some classes. Candice was the fastest sprinter on her high school track team. Usually, the consequence of not attending class was to go to school on Saturday. This would have meant she would miss her track meet.

Solution: I told the school to follow their policy fully. There were no excuses for her behavior, even if she was helping win track meets. Next, I talked with Candice and held her accountable for her actions.

Rationale: She needed to understand that skipping class was not in her best interest. She was the one losing out. One great memory is when Candice went to law school; she told me she would attend all her classes. She felt a responsibility to make sure she learned everything they were teaching so she could better represent her future clients. I thought back to the experience she had in high school.

Behavior (Desired)

As a parent, the way you act sets an example for your child to follow. Your children observe and learn from your every action. To encourage positive behavior, I rewarded the actions I wanted to see repeated with hugs, kisses, compliments, Skittles, or any other reward they valued. Consistently, I modeled the behavior I wished for them to adopt. I made it a point to use "please" and "thank you" regularly, highlighting the joy these simple words bring to others. I practiced proper table manners, using a knife and fork and exhibiting good dining etiquette. I made an effort to speak kindly and respectfully to everyone, treating them with dignity. This wasn't always easy, especially with people I didn't particularly like, but I ensured my children couldn't sense any difference.

Rather than focusing on negative or harmful behavior, my approach was often to ignore it when possible. By not giving attention to undesirable behavior, I found that it often diminished on its own. This method of focusing on and reinforcing positive behavior while calmly managing fewer desirable actions is an effective way to guide children toward constructive habits and attitudes.

Situation 1: One day, when it was just Candice and me at home (Danielle hadn't been born yet), Candice became upset over something she wanted but didn't get. She expressed her frustration by screaming, crying, and flailing on the living room floor. While I was concerned about her safety, I knew it was important not to reinforce this behavior. I discreetly observed from behind a door, out of her sight, to make sure she wouldn't hurt herself. I was uncertain of the best approach but stayed vigilant.

After a short while, Candice looked around for me. Noticing my absence, she calmly stood up and resumed her activities as if nothing had happened. When we interacted again, I chose to act normally, as if the incident hadn't occurred. This experience was a valuable lesson in handling such situations calmly and not reinforcing negative behavior while ensuring the child's safety.

Solution: Ensure you are consistent in what you expect of them. Candice never had another tantrum after that incident. That was a relief because my approach had been effective. I would have followed the same pattern if it had continued, but fortunately, it did not.

Rationale: Remember, there is no punishment for bad behavior, nor is there a reward. However, that doesn't mean there aren't consequences for those actions.

Situation 2: Danielle did not have any tantrums. She had a different personality. She was more subtle with her behaviors. She would pinch me when she was displeased or did not get her way as a small child! I could feel her little fingers giving me soft pinches on my legs, letting me know of her displeasure.

Solution: I knew this behavior would not last when she got older. I ignored it, and eventually, she stopped.

Rationale: I realized that getting upset or frustrated would not be productive. I had to remain consistent and be patient. It wasn't always easy, but purposeful parenting takes work and dedication.

Situation 3: Candice came home from college for one of the spring breaks. I was happy to see her. She seemed to be doing well in school. When she opened her mouth, I noticed a small metal ball at the tip of her tongue. She was eighteen years old at this time.

Solution: A piercing was not something I would have encouraged, but I never said a word! I ignored it, as outlined in my plan. The next time she visited, it was gone.

Rationale: I remember when I was in college and would come home often. I would have stayed away if I saw that my parents were judgmental or controlling. I did not want to hear my parents disapproving of something I was doing. I carefully ensured that both of my girls wanted to come home, but I always stayed true to my plan and handled any unwanted behavior consistently, no matter their age.

Behavior (Social)

While often overlapping, desired and social behavior represent two distinct facets of human interaction. Desired behavior (as just discussed) is an individual's ideal way of acting, shaped by personal values, goals, and ethical standards. It encapsulates how one strives to behave in various situations, reflecting an inner compass of ideal conduct. On the other hand, social behavior is how individuals act in a societal context, influenced by social norms, cultural expectations, and the presence of others. It often involves adapting or modifying one's behavior to fit into a group or meet the expectations of a social setting.

For example, a person might present themselves as outspoken and assertive (desired behavior). Still, in a group setting, they may be more reserved and agreeable (social behavior) to maintain harmony. The interplay between expected and social behavior is crucial in navigating social interactions and personal identity. Balancing these behaviors requires self-awareness and adaptability, ensuring that one's social conduct aligns with personal values while respecting the dynamics of the social environment.

Situation 1: When Candice was in high school, I received a call from her teacher informing me that Candice was not standing and reciting the *Pledge of Allegiance* to the flag, and some of the other classmates stopped as well, following Candice's lead. When she came home, I spoke with her about what the teacher had said because it is always important to ask the child for their thoughts on what has occurred. This future lawyer informed me that this is a free country with freedom of speech, and she does not have to stand and recite the *Pledge of Allegiance*. Of course, she was right. The problem was I would receive a call at my job! I thought about my options.

Solution: Candice is brilliant, so I had to think about how to resolve this quickly. In a desperate move, I gave Candice a choice. I told her that since her decision impacted me, she could stop reciting the *Pledge of Allegiance* when she turned eighteen. In exchange, I would reward her with a thank-you gift for cooperating. She said I could buy her a new blouse. I was happy to do that! The incident did not happen at the school again.

Rationale: Some may see this as bribery, but in my experience, it's all about assessing the situation and developing a sensible solution. If her choice had no impact on me and she would have received the brunt of her decision, things would have been different. I may have told her to make her own choice but to be prepared for possible consequences. My goal was to help her weigh her choices and how they may impact others before making a hasty decision.

Whether we like it or not, we must follow certain societal norms, such as obeying laws and respecting the rights of others. We need to consider that our actions are not always insular but often impact those around us, whether it's school, work, or community. My goal has always been to teach my children to be thoughtful and purposeful when making choices in life and how they may impact themselves and others. Sometimes, we don't have the luxury of doing what we want, when we want, and where we want. Again, it's a matter of thoughtful decision-making.

Situation 2: Sometimes, Danielle did not want to do certain things that I thought were important. It took her nine years to remember to say "please" and "thank you." Occasionally, she did not want to practice the piano in preparation for her lesson. The piano teacher notified me that Danielle must not be practicing because she did not know the material. My point of view was that I was paying all this money for the piano lessons that she wanted.

Solution: I was able to find a way to reward her. She loved Skittles, but candy was not something I typically wanted my girls to have. There were times I had to make exceptions. I would give her Skittles as a reward for practicing the piano and other tasks she was reluctant to do. This worked well, at least for a while.

Rationale: Danielle observed and learned from her big sister as the second child. She knew that I occasionally rewarded positive behavior in various ways, and she was happy with getting candy. It was a learning process for all of us.

Situation 3: One day, I received one of those dreaded calls from the school. This call came from the after-school program. The teacher informed me that Danielle had become the kids' leader, and they only did what Danielle told them to do. The problem was that the teacher had no control over the kids; Danielle did. A conference was scheduled, and I met with the teacher after work one day. The teacher told me that Danielle had usurped her role. I asked her how long this had been going on. She said about three months. I asked her why she was just now telling me. She said that she had tried to fix it but was not making progress. I told her she should have informed me at the beginning. I politely thanked her for letting me know, and I said I would speak with Danielle and resolve the matter.

Solution: When Danielle got in the car, she knew the teacher and I had talked about her behavior. I could see that Danielle thought she was in trouble. Instead, I said, "You go, girl. I am so proud of your leadership skills." We talked about what she was doing, how she could command such loyalty from the kids, and how a talent like that would benefit her later in life.

Rationale: In a situation like this, I did not want to discourage her from having the attributes that a leader possesses; in fact, I tried to encourage that behavior. However, it was again all about decision-making. She needed to manage her leadership skills without the teacher feeling she had lost control. I advised Danielle on how to finesse her leadership talents, which is an important skill to learn. I kept checking with her and the teacher to ensure the problem was resolved. We had no more issues related to Danielle's leadership behavior.

Bonding

Just as you have invested time in understanding and discovering yourself, applying the same dedication to knowing your children is imperative. This journey of bonding with your children, recognizing their evolving personalities, and adapting to their changing needs is a cornerstone of effective parenting.

Children's personalities are not static; they are shaped and reshaped through various stages of their development. The early years are marked by rapid physical and emotional growth, where foundational traits and behaviors are formed. As children grow, they start asserting their individuality, often influenced by their experiences in school and their interactions with peers and adults. It's essential for parents to not only monitor these changes but to understand them. Engaging in regular conversations, showing interest in their activities, and being an active participant helps identify personality shifts.

Children are exposed to a new world of influences when they start school. The role of peers, teachers, and school culture significantly impacts their behavior and outlook. During these years, parents must balance giving their children the space to grow and guiding them through the complexities of social interactions and academic pressures. Regular communication about their school day, understanding their friendships, and being involved in school activities can provide insights into their evolving world.

As children navigate through different stages, they may exhibit behavioral changes. Some of these changes are a natural part of growing up, while others may be red flags signaling deeper issues. Parents need to be observant and discerning. Changes such as withdrawal, aggression, or a sudden drop in academic performance warrant attention. Addressing these issues with empathy, open communication, and, if necessary, professional help can ensure that these changes do not adversely affect the child's development.

Different stages of a child's life require different parenting approaches. The authoritarian style may work for a toddler but is often less effective for a teenager seeking autonomy. Adaptability in parenting style while maintaining consistent values and boundaries is vital. It's about evolving from a caregiver to a guide and, eventually, an adviser.

The parent-child bond is not confined to the early years; it's a lifelong connection. As children become adults, the nature of this relationship transforms. The focus shifts to supporting their independence while being a steady source of love and guidance. This enduring bond is nurtured through respect, mutual understanding, and continued interest in each other's lives.

Bonding with your child is a dynamic and continuous journey that demands patience, understanding, and adaptability. By being attentive to your child's evolving personalities, engaging in their lives, and adapting your parenting approach, you can foster a bond that nurtures your child's development and enriches your relationship with them through all stages of life.

Situation: When my girls were young, monitoring and guiding them was more manageable. Once they were walking and talking and their personalities were evident, then came the challenges. Candice was strong-willed and opinionated. She was naturally bright and did not have to work hard at anything she did. She was always bored whenever she came home. She had good social skills and was considered "delightful." She was an accomplished athlete and musician, playing the violin and piano.

Danielle had what I call a "softer" personality. She was the youngest and could be very charming. She observed her sister's behavior and learned from her what to copy or delete. Danielle excelled in dancing and singing. She played the piano, was a natural leader, and was a joy to be around. She was very studious, worked hard in school, and got good grades.

Solution: I didn't have to take any drastic steps, but I had to realize that knowing myself was an integral part of my plan. I needed to understand and respect each of my girls and be careful not to compare them to each other.

I did not realize that as they got older, their personalities would change so much, and I did not even see it coming at first. Candice was more sensitive than I had ever realized. She had hidden it well with her strong personality. Her personality became less assertive as she got older. Danielle, on the other hand, became more assertive and opinionated. She reminded me more of Candice in her approach to life. Both girls developed a sense of humor when they became adults that I had not seen in them as children. Now, they make me laugh all the time with their witty comments.

Rationale: I had always thought I knew my girls' personalities until I saw how they evolved as they grew up. Awareness of how children develop is essential, and their personalities will likely change. As they change, your PPP may also need to be adjusted. Discipline or other parental methods may need to be altered to achieve the intended result based on their personality.

Childcare

Finding quality childcare that aligns with your parenting style ensures a cohesive and nurturing child development environment. The early years of a child's life are crucial for their overall growth, shaping their social, emotional, and cognitive skills. When childcare providers mirror a parent's values, it creates a consistent framework for the child, reinforcing the same principles, discipline, and care they receive at home. This consistency is essential in fostering a sense of security and trust in young children, which is pivotal for their emotional wellbeing. It also reduces the potential for confusion and mixed messages, allowing the child to understand expectations and boundaries clearly.

While it may be challenging to find, choosing quality childcare that complements your style can significantly contribute to the child's seamless social and behavioral development. It ensures that the child is not only in a safe and caring environment but also actively promotes their learning and development in a manner that resonates with their home life. This can be especially important in language development, problem-solving skills, and social interaction.

Additionally, when parents and childcare providers are on the same page, it fosters a strengthened partnership. This collaboration enables more effective communication regarding the child's progress, challenges, and milestones, ensuring a well-rounded approach to the child's upbringing. Ultimately, choosing a childcare setting is not just about convenience or quality care; it's about creating a cohesive, supportive environment that nurtures a child's development.

Situation: Keeping children safe when others were responsible for them was very difficult for me. The children were finished with school while I was still working, and I could not be home at the time school let out. Fortunately, the public school they attended had an after-school program that was quite helpful. Sometimes, the children needed to participate in extracurricular activities right after school, and I had to find a way to get them there.

Solution: If you need childcare, select a school that provides transportation. Candice wanted to take gymnastics, and a school bus service would pass right by where she wanted to take the class. The school transportation policy for the buses was only to take the kids to the scheduled drop-off spot. I spoke with the administration of the school bus service and asked if they could just let her out at the stop sign because her class was right there. After much pleading, they agreed. Then, I arranged to have her picked up after her gymnastics class.

Rationale: I had little control in this area, which was a real stressor, and I know others, especially today, have a similar issue. Research and preparation can be a time saver. It is always a good idea to ask for what you need. If you can anticipate your needs (school, childcare hours, extracurricular activities), finding a solution that will work for you and your children is much easier. That will ease your stress and some of the parental guilt we feel when someone else is watching our children.

Criticism

Learning to handle criticism, whether in parenting or other aspects of life, is an invaluable skill that fosters personal growth and resilience. When received constructively, criticism can be a powerful tool for self-improvement and reflection. The key lies in distinguishing between constructive feedback and mere negative commentary. Embrace constructive criticism as an opportunity to learn and evolve; it often provides insights you might overlook. Listening actively, keeping an open mind, and avoiding immediate defensive reactions is crucial. Reflect on the feedback objectively, assessing its validity and applicability to your situation.

This might mean considering alternative viewpoints or strategies that could enhance your approach to parenting. It's important to remember that criticism does not reflect your entire character or capabilities but a specific aspect of behavior or decision-making. Developing a thick skin and maintaining a positive attitude toward learning from feedback can significantly improve your parenting style and life skills. Remember, the goal is not to be perfect but to be a better version of yourself, continually adapting and growing. Then, you can be a better parent and role model for your children.

Situation: I remember interviewing for a job where I was responsible for leading a team in building a new hospital. I was excited about this opportunity because I had the expertise and skills that would have been appropriate for this job. Yet, I did not get the job. Consistently, I would ask the people in the recruiting firm why I was not chosen. The response I received was that the lady who interviewed me thought I needed to be more detailed. I had developed a parenting plan that was quite detailed, and I followed it every minute of my life! I was a single parent; I had to be thorough. I even had to count the Skittles for each girl and make sure they had the same color! People say I am the most detail-oriented person they know.

However, another exciting opportunity came along when I interviewed for a job at a company in financial trouble. The people interviewing me were responsible for the financial difficulties and lost revenue. I never had financial problems in any hospital department for which I was responsible. In my personal life, I was very good at managing money. The episode with my parents and the checks they gave me that had expired was a blessing in disguise. Again, I did not get this job. When I asked why I was not considered, I was told they did not think I could manage the finances. Know thyself! That was the last job I interviewed for because I had managed my personal finances so well that I did not even need a job right away (and you can, too).

Solution: Use your experiences to teach your children to know themselves and not let others define them. When you are with your children, you can help them handle criticism like you do by following your PPP. My girls could see I was not disappointed about not getting a particular job.

Criticism from loved ones and family members may be the most difficult to manage. Your family may know you very well. They could be right when they give "constructive" criticism, but that's not always the case. As a trained listener, I paid close attention to their comments. I never got into a heated debate when they said something I did not appreciate. I would thank them for their comments and tell them I will seriously consider what they say. If I felt their comments had merit, I would adjust. If not, I would ignore them.

Rationale: Always consider the source when receiving advice. Knowing yourself and following your PPP can serve as a reminder that just because someone shares an opinion doesn't mean we have to attach value to it. Teaching our children that concept when they are young will help them develop their sense of self and ability to filter out negativity. Showing by example is a subtle way to do that.

Death

Growing up in a funeral home and working as a hospital administrator, I was familiar with sickness, death, and dying. My mother died when my children were relatively young. I told Candice that "Nanny" had died, and the funeral would be in St. Louis. I asked if she wanted to go. Of course, she said yes. As traumatic as it was for me to see my mother lying there, my little girls played with their toys near the casket, seemingly oblivious to the gravity of the situation.

In public, I always hid the grief and devastation I felt. When I was alone, I would let it out. In front of them, I thought I had to be strong. That behavior was likely a result of my upbringing, where death was commonly addressed. I understand that others will probably react differently, and I'm unsure if I should have been more demonstrative with my children regarding the topic. Sometimes, as parents, we can only do our best and hope it's good enough.

Situation: My brother died when my daughters were teenagers. They knew him very well. He was a wonderful brother and uncle. That situation was difficult for me; my two girls knew it hit me hard. I could not hide as much of my grief as I had in the past. I just did the best I could not to traumatize them. I did want them to know that death was a natural end to life and that it was permissible to be sad and miss a loved one. I had to force myself to have these conversations with my girls and tried to be stronger than I felt. I was always concerned about what would happen to them if I died before they became adults. Who was going to take care of them? What if no one follows my wishes?

Solution: As part of my parenting plan, I made sure to have a will that was updated periodically. I wanted to ensure that whatever I had saved would go to them. I used my camcorder and videotaped my final words. In it, I told them how much I loved and wanted the best for them. As they got older, I would sit them down, and we would go over my final wishes. They hated it. "Oh, Mom, do we have to go over that again?" I compiled a notebook; on the cover, it says in bold type, **When I Die**, with everything they need to know. A survivor's guide includes all important papers, like birth certificates, marriage licenses, computer passwords, investments, names of friends to contact, funeral home and cemetery, etc.

Rationale: This is not a task that anyone finds pleasant, but it must be done not for you but for your loved ones. Even with my background, my brother's death had a devastating effect on me and my girls. So, I always prepared for what should be done if I died, but I made sure I talked to them more often about the details. They know I want to ease their burden as much as possible when my time comes. They will not have to wonder what to do for me. It may be uncomfortable, but I firmly believe that preparation is critical. With your family, death should be handled as any other unavoidable situation. Discuss it, prepare for it, and then move on with enjoying the rest of your life.

Decision-making

As children mature, it's crucial for them to sense a degree of autonomy in their lives. Achieving this was a key objective of mine. I endeavored to ensure they perceived opportunities for making choices. For example, during grocery shopping, I would offer them options, asking whether they preferred chicken or fish. These minor choices helped them psychologically, giving them a feeling of being involved and that their views were valued. Encouraging them to make sound decisions from a young age was a strategy to equip them for more significant choices later in life. As they reach adolescence, the stakes of their decisions increase, potentially leading to serious repercussions if poor choices are made. This is why maintaining a balance is vital. While I needed to protect their health and safety, preventing overly risky decisions, I also strived to offer them as much freedom as possible. My aim was for them not to perceive me as excessively protective.

Reflecting on my own teenage years, I recall how my parents permitted me to attend parties, including the memorable "blue light in the basement" gatherings. These events were the highlight of my social life. Going to college later, I felt I had enjoyed my youth without excessive restrictions. In contrast, some of my freshman peers seemed to overindulge in newfound freedom, staying up all night playing cards, neglecting studies, and eventually dropping out. This seemed to stem from a lack of experience in making prudent decisions. While I still enjoyed parties and dating in college, I balanced these with adequate rest and study.

This personal history informed my approach to my children. I wanted them to develop sound decision-making skills, so I consciously allowed them as much autonomy in their choices as possible. Understanding that mistakes and the consequences they bring are vital in life's learning process, I emphasized to them the value of learning from errors. Everyone errs, but the key lies in the lessons learned from these mistakes. The most accomplished individuals have all made missteps. Experiencing the repercussions of less-than-ideal choices at a young age imparts a crucial life lesson. It was my hope that their early decisions wouldn't involve critical situations where parental intervention would still be necessary.

Situation 1: When Candice was eight years old, she expressed a desire to attend a music camp in Michigan; I took the necessary steps to make it happen despite the considerable expense and eight-week duration. My family advised against it, citing her young age and lack of experience being away from home for such an extended period. They feared it wouldn't be beneficial for her. However, faced with this challenging decision, I prioritized Candice's wishes. She was the one eager to attend, and as a parent, I wanted to support her choice, especially since she was a beginner violinist.

To ease the financial burden, I applied for a scholarship for Candice, but the camp initially denied it, stating they typically awarded scholarships to high school students. Undeterred, I wrote back, advocating for Candice's potential as a violinist, and requested them to reconsider. There's no harm in persistently pursuing what you want. Surprisingly, the camp responded, asking for an audio tape of Candice playing the violin. Although her violin teacher was skeptical about Candice's chances and hesitant to assist, I was adamant. With my encouragement, Candice practiced a Suzuki piece, which we recorded on an audio tape and sent to Interlochen. Ultimately, the camp awarded her a partial scholarship, enough to make attending financially feasible.

During Candice's time at the camp, I accepted a job in another state. This meant that Candice would not return to her familiar home. I informed her that we would relocate to our new house by the end of her camp. I promised to take videos of our old home to ease the transition and asked her preferences for the new house. Candice's wish was for her own room, a request I gladly fulfilled, ensuring she could choose first.

Solution: I had a great deal of nerve asking for a scholarship to a world-renowned camp for an eight-year-old who had only been taking lessons for less than a year, but I did it because I could see that she had talent that needed to be developed (that is a mother for you!). I informed her that she had talent even though her violin teacher had her doubts.

Rationale: I knew this was the right place for my daughter, but I wanted to ensure she did not feel isolated. To make sure, I would visit the camp to check on her, and she would cry when I left. After we moved, it was an exhausting 17½ hour drive to her camp, but I made the trip at least four times to ensure she knew we would still visit her. In week seven, I received a call from Candice stating she had auditioned for the final recital and made it! There was no crying or homesickness evident in her voice. She returned to that camp for three more years, and the homesickness never returned.

Situation 2: Danielle decided that she wanted to be a teacher. My grandfather and father were high school teachers, so I understand this honorable profession. My only concern was that she may not be able to afford the lifestyle I knew she wanted on a teacher's salary.

Solution: I sat with Danielle, took a piece of paper, and divided it into two columns. On the left side of the paper was a teacher's income, and on the right was the cost of the lifestyle she wanted. A teacher's income was well below what she would need.

Undeterred, she eventually became a teacher, and her first job was with Teach for America. After graduating with a bachelor's degree, that organization trains teachers to work with underprivileged children. She thoroughly enjoyed that experience. Her teaching method dramatically increased the test scores for her class. The endless hours of going over homework with me when she was a school-age child may have helped her be a good teacher. She understood how to motivate children to learn.

Rationale: I did not continue discussing her career choice; my only responsibility was to ensure she considered all the facts. After that, it was up to her to employ the decision-making skills she had learned to make her own choices over the years.

Delegating

Mastering the art of delegating responsibilities is a critical step for parents to effectively manage their time and well-being. It's essential to acknowledge that seeking help is not a sign of inadequacy but rather a wise strategy to maintain a balanced and healthy family life. Delegating allows parents to take necessary breaks, focus on other essential aspects of life, and return to their parenting duties rejuvenated.

Finding trustworthy and competent individuals or services that align with your parenting philosophy and values is critical. Family members, friends, professional childcare providers, or reputable childcare facilities. Communicate your child's routines, needs, and expectations to ensure consistent care. It's crucial to gradually build a sense of comfort and trust with the caregivers, allowing you to step back confidently. Remember, delegating childcare does not diminish your role as a parent; instead, it empowers you to manage your responsibilities more effectively and provides your child with valuable socializing experiences and exposure to diverse, caring environments.

Situation 1: Danielle had extracurricular activities twice a week. I could not take her, and the bus route would not work.

Solution: I contacted all the mothers and offered to pay them to take Danielle with their children. I decided it was best to pay them because I didn't have the time to share in carpooling duties. This worked out successfully. Another resource I was able to tap into was a transportation service called "Kids Cab." This was a van that would take kids to their activities.

Rationale: The arrangement worked, and I was grateful that I could schedule this resource to take my girls to their activities as a last resort. I used Kids Cab to get them to their lessons and activities when I had no other resource available.

Situation 2: Both girls took piano lessons. This was another challenge for me. The piano teacher taught at specific times after school. There was no way that I could get them to the school where the piano teacher gave her lessons. They were too young to drive themselves.

Solution: I contacted the teacher and asked if she could come to my home and give my two children their lessons. She said she would. This was wonderful. The kids could take the bus home on the day they had piano lessons, come to the house, be there with an adult, and take their lessons. By the time the lessons were over, the babysitter would have arrived. The piano teacher could give and supervise their lessons so they would not be alone in the house.

Rationale: This not only benefited them but allowed me to continue working. I breathed another sigh of relief at this double dose of delegation.

Situation 3: There were times that I needed to go out of town for a job responsibility or have meetings early in the morning or after work. I needed people I could trust to be with my children when leaving town. This situation caused me so much stress. Finding trustworthy people was difficult, especially when my children were young.

Solution: I was fortunate enough to have two first cousins who worked as nurses. When I had to take a work trip, I offered each of them an all-expense-paid trip to my home to care for my two girls. They were eager to comply. One came for one journey, and the other came for another. I felt comfortable with them because they were family, nurses, good cooks, and had raised adult children. Spending time with them before and after my trips was also lovely.

Rationale: At times, as a parent, you may find yourself in a position where delegating the responsibility of your children becomes necessary. This is a common challenge faced by all parents and should not be associated with feelings of inadequacy or failure. Our actions are often guided by what is best for our family. Recognizing your limitations and choosing individuals who are skilled in managing specific scenarios can significantly simplify your life. Since every situation is unique, it's important to seek a solution that is well-suited to your needs. It's crucial to ask for assistance when required. You shouldn't feel hesitant or uneasy about assigning tasks to others that you are unable to handle yourself.

Difficult Situations

Navigating difficult situations with children often involves balancing their desire for independence and parental guidance, as exemplified by my experience when my daughters became teenagers. Since

Candice was the first to turn sixteen, both of us were learning along the way. Most issues arose from her desire for more autonomy, based on her belief that responsible behavior as a daughter and student warranted greater freedom.

Situation 1: Candice's father had given her a car, enabling her to manage her and Danielle's extracurricular activities independently. Her sense of independence was further bolstered by her part-time job, through which she earned her own money. Meanwhile, my work schedule prevented me from being available to drive them to their various activities. This situation presented a complex challenge: acknowledging Candice's maturity and accomplishments while maintaining appropriate parental boundaries and guidance.

Solution: This was one of those pivotal moments when I knew and understood that things were changing. The dynamic was going to be different, and the solution was simple. I could either get on board or torment myself by trying to take control of the inevitable. It was simple: I had to learn to let go.

Rationale: Such scenarios are common in parenting teenagers, requiring a delicate balance between empowering them and ensuring their safety and well-being. Sometimes, as parents, we have to recognize when to interfere and when to take a step back, which is not an easy thing to do.

Situation 2: One afternoon, I said, "You are living in my house, and you must abide by my rules." I am not sure that I should have ever said this, but I did! Candice said she would not do so, packed her suitcase, and left the house! I did not know where she was. I had to think about how I should handle it. I contacted the police and filed a missing child report. They said they could do nothing because she was sixteen years old. How can a sixteen-year-old not meet the legal guidelines of a missing child? She did not back down about the house rules, nor did I. She still had keys to the house and promised Danielle that she would continue to take her to all her activities. We were at a standstill for weeks.

Solution: I would go to the shoe store where she worked and talk with her, letting her know we missed her and that she was essential to Danielle and me. She was part of our family, and we wanted her to return home. I reminded her that she would be leaving to go to college in less than a year, and by working together, we could make the transition from home to college easier. She also knew I would only pay for her college education if she came home. Eventually, she agreed, and we were able to get back together.

Rationale: We were both committed to resolving our issues, and we succeeded. I discovered that she had been living with her friend's family, where the family thought she had been neglected and her single parent mother was frequently absent, and she needed a place to stay. Surprisingly, the family never reached out to me to verify these assumptions. However, after Candice returned home, I took the initiative to contact them and explained the actual situation. Naturally, they felt embarrassed once they were made aware of the real circumstances. Although it was a challenging period, I believe that it led to a deeper mutual understanding between me and my daughter.

Situation 3: An incident occurred after I invited my cousin, Sharon, from Flint, MI, to Marietta, GA, to look after my daughters while I was away on a work trip. Sharon bonded wonderfully with my girls during her stay. She's an exceptional cook, so they enjoyed delicious meals. Upon my return, Sharon happily reported that they behaved like little angels. While Sharon and I were chatting in the kitchen, Candice approached and asked if she could attend a party, hoping to extend her curfew to stay out as late as she desired. This request caught me off guard, and I remained composed as I contemplated how to respond. Candice was clever in choosing this moment, thinking she might have a better chance of getting her way in Sharon's presence. However, I knew that I couldn't agree to her request.

Solution: Sharon watched with an expression of disbelief, curious about how the situation would unfold. I addressed Candice with a series of questions, probing into why she felt it was necessary to stay out beyond her curfew and if she understood the risks associated with being out alone all night. As the conversation progressed, fortune seemed to be on my side; Candice eventually agreed to return home on time. Throughout this exchange, I maintained my composure and focused on persuading her to adhere to her curfew.

Rationale: I have no idea what would have happened if she did not change her mind. I did not like the attempted manipulation, especially after just having returned from a long trip. Later, Sharon said she admired how I handled the situation. Sometimes, parents do get lucky! This is when I remembered my plan and remained calm.

Divorce

After completing my college education, I pursued further coursework to become a marriage counselor. Once certified, I gained a deep understanding of what constitutes both good and bad marriages. However, following the birth of Candice, I realized that my own marriage exhibited several unfavorable traits. My husband was undoubtedly a good man; he was intelligent, supported me during my studies, and was diligent and successful in his career. Yet, our values and aspirations were misaligned. Acknowledging this, we mutually decided to part ways amicably. At the time of our divorce, Candice was three years old, and Danielle was just an infant. Despite the separation, Paul and I maintained a civil relationship. He remained involved in the children's lives, attending their birthdays, sporting activities, and other events.

Being a single parent meant bearing all responsibilities alone, which felt like being a "middle card" in a deck. Tasks such as taking out the garbage, picking up the children from daycare, and supervising them when I needed rest fell solely on me. Danielle seemed to adapt without visible effects, while Candice experienced brief bouts of sadness, missing her father, who, along with his new wife, Michelle, was still in Michigan.

Nonetheless, I chose to focus on the positive aspects. There was one less barrier to executing my plans; I didn't need to consult with another person in the household who might disagree with my decisions. Furthermore, the children couldn't play one parent against the other to get their way. Our home was peaceful, and I was fully in charge, steering the family according to my vision.

Situation: One of the key challenges I faced in raising my two daughters was the lack of a male presence in our home, particularly that of an African American man. This absence concerned me, as I believed it might leave them less equipped to understand and interact with men as they got older. This situation presented a unique obstacle in their upbringing, one that I couldn't resolve alone, and it was a factor I considered significant in their development and understanding of diverse perspectives.

Solution: I got them involved with co-ed activities where male role models might be present. They spent a lot of time with my brother until he passed. I also had married friends who visited periodically, and my daughters got to see their dynamics. Of course, none of that would replace having a male role model in the home. Still, I did my best to ensure the hand I was dealt was a winner, not a loser.

Rationale: Their father did an excellent job maintaining consistent contact with his children, significantly improving the situation for everyone involved. It was crucial for us to avoid any display of bitterness, shouting, displeasure, or any behavior that might worry the children. I made a conscious effort never to speak negatively about their father in their presence. Speaking ill of your children's father serves no purpose, especially when they hold him in high regard. He was an exceptional ex-husband. Similarly, I harbored no negative feelings toward his girlfriend, Michelle. After they married, Michelle and I developed a relationship akin to sisters. I liked her, and the feeling was mutual. When I relocated from Michigan to Georgia, and they moved to Florida, Michelle was comfortable with Paul coming to Georgia to assist with my home maintenance tasks. His visits were always a pleasure; he would fix things and spend quality time with his daughters.

I recall a conversation with Michelle where she shared that some of her friends were puzzled about how she could send her husband to stay at his ex-wife's house. Her response was light-hearted yet telling: "It is the safest place for him!" This exemplified the closeness of our relationship. She knew I had no romantic interest in him anymore. Michelle and I would travel together, talk on the phone frequently, and share details of our lives. We found we had much in common. When the girls visited, she was like a second mother to them. I greatly appreciated the love and care she showed my daughters.

One particular act of kindness from Michelle that remains dear to me involved her selflessness in caring for my children. On one occasion, she flew to Marietta to allow me to go on a tennis trip with my friends to Hilton Head. Upon my return, she revealed that her grandfather had passed away during my trip, but she chose not to tell me until I was back so as not to spoil my vacation. She then left to be with her family in Tennessee. Her considerate action deeply touched me and still brings tears to my eyes.

Driving

In the section about "difficult situations," I briefly mentioned driving, but I believe this topic warrants further discussion due to its significance in everyone's life. A major question for parents is determining when their teenagers are mature enough to drive. How can one be sure of their maturity level? This decision felt like a matter of life and death to me, especially given the well-known stories of young drivers making poor choices with tragic outcomes. The need for my daughters to drive arose from my job's constraints, which prevented me from being available to take them to their extracurricular activities. Allowing them to drive themselves would be incredibly helpful, but how could I address my concerns for their safety?

Throughout their lives, my parenting approach included imparting fundamental lessons to prepare them for significant milestones, and learning to drive was no exception. For each daughter, I began their driving education in a school parking lot, covering basics like starting the car, using the gears, accelerating, braking, etc., while simultaneously assessing their readiness. I strongly advocate for enlisting professional driving instructors to ensure your children learn safe driving practices when they reach the legal driving age. This decision was pivotal for their safety and, frankly, for my peace of mind.

Receiving cars at age sixteen for both of my girls was a double-edged sword. On the positive side, having cars meant they could independently attend all their practices, which was incredibly beneficial. Another advantage was the control it gave them over their mobility. Without their own cars, they might have ended up as passengers in vehicles driven by less adequately trained drivers. I also made it a practice to leave money in a drawer for their activity-related expenses, as I might not be home when they needed it. Raised with a sense of responsibility, they would always inform me about how much money they required and only took what was necessary. The negative aspect, however, was the freedom it gave them to go anywhere with anyone, leaving me uncertain about their whereabouts and activities. (This was before the age of cell phones and GPS tracking devices.)

Situation 1: Both girls were told not to drive downtown or go to places unrelated to their authorized activities. I knew that they probably would drive to those parts of town without my knowing about it. That is reality. They thought I would never find out. This is when I hoped having followed my plan all these years would keep them safe and give them sound judgment. It was working as I'd hoped until I received a call from a friend who said she saw Danielle at a mall in a part of the city I'd told her not to visit.

Solution: This was another instance where I decided less is more. I chose not to say anything to Danielle about what I had heard. I would always warn her about staying watchful and avoiding dangerous situations and locations, so I had to trust that she would, but I also asked my friend to tell me if she saw her at that mall again.

Rationale: I knew that I couldn't monitor them forever, and the best way to go for me was to make sure they understood why I made certain rules. I found that sometimes, the best approach to handle a situation was to monitor it and wait, which was not always easy for me.

Situation 2: Candice told me she was going to a party with one of her classmates and understood that she had a curfew. I knew the family, so I allowed her to go, but for some reason, I still felt uncomfortable.

Solution: My intuition told me to call the parents. When I did, I found out they were not having a party and, in fact, had not seen Candice in weeks. After she got home safe and sound, I asked her how the party was at this family's home. She said it was fine. Then I told her that I had called the family, there was no party, and they had not seen her. Do you then know what she said? "Busted." I took her phone privileges away for a week, but I had no way to monitor if she was staying off the phone, so that may not have been the best choice. I don't remember ever finding out where she went.

Rationale: By following a parenting plan all their lives, I think there is a greater probability that children will be ready to not only drive but also to make wise choices. Let's face it: they are always going to test the waters. This situation reinforced my belief that if you tell them not to do something, that is the very thing they will do, so be prepared. There will be times when you won't get the whole truth, but there can still be consequences for their actions. However, remember, if you can't monitor the punishment, it is wiser not to dole it out.

Faith

All through my life, I spent a great deal of time in church. Seeing familiar faces, listening to the preacher give the sermon, and singing in the choir fulfilled and energized me. My nuclear family and grandmother were also very active in the church. I wanted that same experience for my two girls because it is essential to give them a sense of how to live life believing in God. Knowing that we are not alone and have a heavenly father who can help us through life is essential. What a challenge it ended up being.

Situation 1: The church I attended as a child always allowed children of any age to be in the main sanctuary with everyone else. The parent usually took the child out if a baby cried or a toddler misbehaved. Sometimes, the preacher would say it is better to have the child in church crying than not in the church at all. That is what I was used to. I was hoping to find that when looking for a church home so my children could have a faith-based life.

I'd heard good things about a local church, so I visited with my girlfriend, Karmen, and my two-year-old. Candice sat quietly in a chair next to me and Karmen. A deacon came to me and said a childcare center was a block away where I could leave Candice during the church service. There was no way I was going to do that! I did not know who was supervising the children, and I wanted Candice with me anyway. I politely said no, I would keep Candice with me. The deacon returned and told us the seats were for adults, not children. Would I put Candice in my lap so an adult could have that seat? Candice was not the type of child that would sit on my lap. Again, I refused to put Candice in my lap and explained my reasoning to him. As you might have guessed, I was getting quite annoyed. The deacon returned a third time and said if I didn't give up Candice's seat, I would have to leave!

Solution: I could have delegated my children's care to a nearby daycare, but that's not what I wanted for my family. I couldn't believe this was how I was treated in a church. I found other churches with similar rules about not having a child in the main sanctuary.

Rationale: That experience was new to me, and I eventually gave up my search. I did not want to be in a church that upset me because of their policies. I did not want a church to turn me into a big sinner.

Situation 2: As the children got older, Danielle became interested in faith, and as a young teen, she read a Bible chapter before she went to sleep. I don't know many teenagers who do that, so I told her how special that was. When she finished reading the entire Bible, I congratulated her on this accomplishment. What was so upsetting to me was the difficulty finding a church where I could take my children with me to the sanctuary. I just had to find a way for us to attend church together.

Solution: Even though I could not find the ideal church home, I wanted them to have faith-based lives, so I decided to delegate. We were living in Detroit, MI, and I had family that lived close. So, I asked my aunt and uncle to take the children to church on Sunday mornings. They were so happy to oblige, and my girls not only went to church but could also spend time with family.

Rationale: Sometimes, life does not go as we might like it to, but with a bit of patience, eventually, things can work out.

Finances

When your PPP is being developed and implemented, consideration must be given to finances and affordability. Having enough money to execute my plan was of considerable concern to me. What if I got sick and could not care for them or myself? What if I lost my job? The "what ifs" probably would not be under my control, but there were actions I could take at least to prepare, prevent, or manage these adverse situations financially.

Situation 1: I never wanted my children to support me in my old age. Being a financial burden on them would have been the worst thing that could have happened to me.

Solution: In my early twenties, I self-funded a life insurance policy, a disability policy, and investments not associated with a job. I wanted to be prepared if an adverse situation occurred and I was unemployed or did not have enough money when I truly needed it.

Rationale: Thinking back to my childhood experiences when I could not cash those checks my parents had given me, I learned the importance of understanding finance. I had learned that I needed to make my way and not depend on gifts. Even at Bible Study, my grandmother taught us how to open a bank account. Her slogan was to "spend some and save some for a rainy day." I followed that mindset and started saving as much money as possible from my part-time and summer jobs during my teenage years.

Situation 2: As a single parent, after I paid for food, clothing, utilities, insurance, mortgage, gas for the car, and other necessities, there were times when I couldn't afford my girls' extracurricular activities. They were cheerleading, gymnastics, dance, horseback riding, swimming, cross country, track, playing violin and piano, and all of them required time and money.

Solution: I consciously decided not to let that situation depress me. I didn't have time to be sad or complain and would instead focus on a solution. So, I went into action. I thought about the financial section of my plan and cut back on anything I could. I sometimes found loose change in the car, pockets, drawers, etc. Every little bit helped. I shopped at discount stores and bought as much as possible in bulk, and all entertainment that cost money was put on hold. Eating one piece of chicken instead of my usual two would allow me to have it for dinner the next day. One of the reasons I drink so much water to this day is because I gave up drinking anything that cost extra money. The water from the faucet was okay with me. Packing lunches for the children instead of giving them money to buy lunch at school was implemented successfully many times when I needed to save more money. The benefit was knowing that the lunch I packed for them was healthy.

Rationale: Being able to change my lifestyle took effort, but it was worth it, and I developed lifelong, healthy behaviors as well.

Situation 3: My good friend Poppy and I met in Jack and Jill of America, Inc., an organization dedicated to nurturing African American children through leadership development and volunteer service. The members were responsible for paying dues, attending meetings, and planning monthly activities for children in their respective age groups. Poppy was well-versed in financial matters. I learned about the stock market and how to invest money, which was helpful to me. She continues to guide me even to this day. However, sometimes, money was tight, and I had to make difficult decisions that did not always align with my financial plan.

Solution: There were occasions when I had to temporarily reduce the amount that I had instructed my employer to take out of my check for retirement. Since they matched what I put in, I never liked to reduce it, but the lesson is that we do what we have to for our family.

A last resort was to pull money from my savings accounts. That was a difficult choice to make because I had always been such a proponent of saving money. I did not want to get into the habit of withdrawing cash because that would deplete my savings for other emergencies.

I had already given up on anything unnecessary regarding entertainment, expensive clothes, dinner, etc. I got most of my groceries and household goods at warehouse clubs. I occasionally bought a gallon-sized bottle of wine, but that was rare. I tried to avoid fast food, soda pop, sweets, and unhealthy foods. Often, I would prepare large meals on Sunday and heat them throughout the week.

The Dollar Store was one of my favorite places to shop. I would buy things like kitchen utensils, greeting cards, and office supplies. I felt I had gotten my money's worth when I left the store. I learned to entertain myself by watching movies, reading books from the library, and doing things that did not require much money.

Rationale: My motto is to plan for the worst and hope for the best. Being frugal wasn't a choice for me; it was necessary, but practical fiscal habits emerged. I hoped that providing for my children as a single mom would teach them that obstacles can be overcome with patience and persistence.

Situation 4: When Candice was a baby, she got a terrible red rash all over her body. I was concerned and called the pediatrician, who could not make an appointment until later that week. For three days, I watched her to ensure I did not have to go to the emergency room. I was anxious, not knowing how severe the rash was. Once I took her to the pediatrician, the rash had disappeared. The doctor called it "roseola." After being charged for the visit, I fumed in the car. I could have saved the office visit charge by waiting one more day. I could have used that money elsewhere.

Solution: I had to stop and think about the situation. I realized I should be happy. Would I have felt I got my money's worth if my daughter's condition had worsened? Would I have been happier if the pediatrician had to admit her to the hospital for a severe illness? I learned my lesson, and never again would I be furious if I received good news, even if my budget took a hit.

Rationale: Always remember as parents that money well spent is an acceptable outcome.

Forgiveness

For most of my life, I could keep feelings of regret and guilt to a minimum. As stated in my plan, I was especially aware of avoiding these two nonproductive feelings. However, one regret has stayed with me.

Situation 1: When Danielle was three years old, she asked if she could take piano lessons. I thought she was too young, and I did not have a piano. Two years went by. On her fifth birthday, she asked, "Mommy, can I take piano lessons now?" For the last two years, she has been waiting to ask! I felt guilt and regret. I had not followed my plan and discounted what she asked me. I did not listen. I was focused on what was important to me, not what she wanted. I was mortified!

Solution: I decided to commit, so I bought a piano and found a teacher. To my delight, she took piano lessons for years. To this day, there is a pain in my heart for not listening to my three-year-old.

Rationale: As I was having a Zoom meeting with my adult girls, I recounted this story as my biggest regret, yet Danielle did not remember any of it. Candice said, "Mom, if this is your biggest regret, you do not have to think about this anymore!" That helped to remind me that it does no good to waste energy on regrets. Guilt can drain energy for years with no purpose. Make peace with your decisions, learn from them if necessary, and move on.

Situation 2: At one point, Danielle didn't want to practice the piano as needed for the year-end recitals. She was a young teenager and was losing her focus. Is this the same child who wanted piano lessons so desperately? Interests do change, and I had to adjust to that fact. I had hoped that she would continue to take lessons so that she could play in orchestras, at parties, or for church choirs.

Solution: I wanted her to play at least for the recitals her piano teachers planned every year. Then, I discovered a simple motivation. Giving her Skittles candies. While it wasn't a permanent fix, it worked for a while. Eventually, she stopped taking piano lessons, and I quietly had to accept her decision. I realized that I was more concerned about what I wanted to do than listening to her.

Rationale: It's crucial to actively listen to your child. Engage in conversations and ask questions that help you understand if your child is making a well-considered decision. Then, trust their judgment and let go. Time has a remarkable ability to ease the stress of such moments. Adopt a mindset that focuses on the positives, as dwelling on mistakes isn't productive. The key is to learn from these experiences.

Sometimes, you might not realize where you've fallen short until your child points it out. For instance, Danielle later confessed to me that there were times when she didn't feel like practicing piano. To circumvent this, she would record herself playing on the keyboard, a technique her teacher used for duets and recital preparations. When she didn't want to practice, she would play the recording so that it sounded like she was engaged in her practice session from her room. This story highlights an essential parenting truth: you can't control everything. The hope is that these little schemes your child concocts are harmless, and as a parent, you do your best to guide them.

Healthy Habits

To encourage your child to embrace healthy eating and exercise habits, you must seize every opportunity to educate them through your actions. Leading by example is the most impactful method of instilling these values. As a parent, you can demonstrate healthy habits by sharing your food choices and exercise routines with them. In my experience, I fostered healthy eating habits in my daughters by mostly avoiding fast food and opting for nutritious meals that included vegetables, poultry, fish, and healthy beverages. We steered clear of soda and desserts, which was made easier by my lack of interest in baking. Additionally, I always encouraged their participation in school sports activities, providing them with ample opportunities to stay active and develop a love for exercise.

Situation: One challenge was the schools they attended. I noticed that the teachers tended to reward the children with sweets like candy, cookies, and donuts.

Solution: To cut down on the sugary treats that tempted the students, including my children, I completed a medical form that asked what allergies my children had. I finished the form by writing that my children were allergic to sweets. That was fortuitous!

Rationale: Interestingly, my girls had always wondered why they did not get the same treats as some of the other kids but had no idea I had instructed the school not to give them sugar treats. They didn't figure out what I had done until they were adults.

Homework

Instilling good homework habits in children is crucial for fostering lifelong study skills. Reflecting on my own high school experience, I realize that I didn't receive much help or reminders from my parents regarding my homework. Despite this, I gravitated toward completing my assignments independently, without needing guidance or support. This personal experience highlights the variability in children's needs for homework assistance and underscores the importance of teaching them effective study habits from an early age.

Situation 1: My two girls were not that happy about doing homework during their early school years. They did not have my dedication to studying. I would come home from work very tired, but I knew I needed to help them with their homework. The goal was to get them in bed by 8:00 p.m. unless they had an activity that required them to go to bed later.

Solution: I would sit with each child and assist them in doing their homework. I made them read the captions under the pictures and the footnotes, if any, and I had them focus on the material. They thought I was "over the top." Even if they received an A on the assignment with a grade of 95, I would sit with them and figure out what they got wrong and how they could have gotten 100. I praised them for doing so well, but we still went over the other 5% so that they would know it the next time.

Rationale: In college, I tutored in statistics and math. Those subjects weren't my strengths, but I had worked hard to understand them and was able to help others. I often tutored graduate students who were used to having passing grades throughout their years in school. They were struggling now and could not understand why. In working with them, I found that many had become complacent and lacked the motivation to master an unfamiliar subject. There was an accumulative effect. All the ones they may have gotten wrong were now facing them because they had never thought about correcting their mistakes if they passed. I remembered this when Candice and Danielle were doing homework. I knew I could prevent them from having this struggle in their lives.

Situation 2: Danielle had always had difficulty with math. How math was taught to the masses in public school was not working for her.

Solution: I could not help her with geometry and trigonometry, so I found an excellent tutor. Every Monday evening, I took Danielle to the math tutor, and then Candice and I would sit in the car and do homework. When Danielle went to college, she took Precalculus and Calculus and got A's in both classes! That was truly amazing!

Rationale: Math did not come easily for me. I can remember trying to understand what Calculus was. Even when reading the definition, I struggled to grasp the concept myself. Danielle's hard work to improve her math skills also paid off. That is why it is so important to know what your child needs. Sometimes, the education they receive in the classroom does not work for everyone. That does not mean your child is not intelligent or cannot learn. It just means they learn differently. Be aware if your child needs more individualized attention. Finding a tutor may be the answer. She always had a positive attitude about being tutored. I made sure of that!

Involvement

It's important for parents to consistently demonstrate interest in their child's activities and experiences despite the challenge of balancing this with a busy schedule, including tiring workdays. Children greatly benefit from knowing their parents care about their personal life and involvement in external activities. This engagement plays a crucial role in their emotional well-being and development.

Situation: My children had a lot of interests and talents. That meant I had to take them to activities or arrange to get them there. Having a job with unpredictable hours made that challenging.

Solution: I became a robot to handle increasing activities while juggling a career. I would press the "automatic button" in my head and do what I had to do. There was no time to think about anything but the task at hand. There was no time to be anxious, no time to be stressed, no time to do anything but what I had to do. It did not matter what had happened at my job. It did not matter that I was tired. I'd always put a smile on my face when I returned home.

Rationale: It was unfair to burden my children with my trials and tribulations at work. I wanted them to know I was glad to see them. In my robot mode, we did homework every evening. I had a child on each side and went from one to the other. They were rolling their eyes often. Later, in college, they had great study habits and did well. They appreciated that they learned excellent study skills from doing homework with me.

It was always a pleasure to hear them play music, the piano and the violin. I viewed this as musical homework. Every day, they had to practice their lessons. I was not always available to listen because of work, but the babysitter ensured that they practiced. Whenever I could get home in time, I would listen and praise them for their progress. This I thoroughly enjoyed. I would usually record their practice and concerts and watch them to this day. My camcorder was always ready to capture these moments. I attended most of their activities, visited their classrooms, attended parent and teacher meetings, etc. They always knew I would be there to watch them and support them in their activities.

Judgment (Parental)

Teaching children good judgment skills is an indispensable aspect of their development, equipping them with the ability to make wise decisions throughout their lives. Good judgment involves assessing situations critically, understanding consequences, and making choices that align with one's values and goals. By instilling these skills, parents empower their children to navigate complex situations, resist peer pressure, and avoid harmful behaviors. This education begins at home through open conversations, real-life examples, and guided decision-making opportunities. Encouraging children to think independently, weigh pros and cons, and consider the impact of their actions helps them develop a solid moral compass.

Good judgment skills are about avoiding adverse outcomes, seizing positive opportunities, and making choices that lead to personal growth and fulfillment. Ultimately, teaching children to think judiciously is a gift that prepares them for the challenges and choices of adulthood. You can have some assurance that your well-developed and implemented PPP will be your guide.

Situation 1: One very challenging episode concerned Candice and Dr. Martin Luther King's famous speech. She was probably five years old and had learned the words "I Have a Dream." She was on the program to give that speech at a Jack and Jill family get-together. A few days before the event, Candice told me she did not want to give a speech in front of people. She appeared to be quite frightened of the possibility. The dilemma for me was, what should I do? Should I tell her that she did not have to give the speech even though she said she would? What message would I be giving her – that she could get out of carrying out her responsibility even though a commitment had been made? Would sharing this speech in front of people traumatize her for life if I forced her to give the speech?

Solution: I agonized over what to do and decided to reason with her. We talked about it. She listened to me, and I to her. We discussed the pros and cons of giving the speech. I tried to understand why she did not want to do it. I told her that nothing bad happens when you address an audience. She already knew there would be no punishment if she decided not to give the speech. Finally, I leaned toward letting her out of that commitment, but before I could say it, she decided she would give the speech! What a relief! I still have that speech on video and have watched it over the years. She also shows that performance to her children, so she must be proud that she did it.

Rationale: Sometimes, you can only do your best when your kids present you with their own ideas. You don't have to have all the answers. You can "wing it;" trust your intuition. After all, being a parent is not about being perfect.

Situation 2: I remember one of the earlier episodes when Candice was under two years old. She was not speaking in complete sentences and could tell you what she wanted with one or two words. As always, I had gotten up early to fix her breakfast. If I fed her first, I could enjoy my meal in peace. That morning, she asked for more juice while I finished cooking my bacon and eggs. I said, "Candice, I will give you more juice as soon as I finish cooking." I had a habit of always listening and responding so she would know my reasoning. She did not like my answer and started shouting, "JUICE! JUICE!" Her face was red, and she was clearly angry. As soon as my breakfast was cooked, I put my plate on the table. Then I went to the refrigerator and poured her more juice. She took her juice and poured it over my breakfast. Why didn't she drink it? The first thing I said to myself was, did she do this purposefully? Was this an accident? Can a child that young retaliate when she does not get her way? How did she even think to pour it on my food? She could have just thrown the juice on the floor. I really could not process it. Once she had ruined my breakfast, she went to the next room to play.

Solution: I decided not to focus more on her actions. Even though she was very young, I was afraid this might set a bad precedent, but I went with my intuition. It would be best to move past this issue, not make a big deal about it, and hope it did not recur.

Rationale: If it did happen again, I would have to deal with it head-on, but this time, I would not give it any more energy or attention. I made the best of my breakfast and went on with my day. Thankfully, it never happened again.

Situation 3: Candice was in middle school and was unhappy with some of my rules. She informed me that she would report me to Child Protective Services (CPS).

Solution: I asked her why that was necessary and if we could work through this ourselves. I was very calm and handled this situation like an administrator. She was determined to make the call, so I decided to facilitate. I asked her if she had the phone number, and she didn't. I gave it to her and wished her well. She had that option if she changed her mind. She decided not to make the phone call.

Rationale: That was the last time she used that manipulative strategy. This is a situation when you call their bluff. What would I have done if she had called protective services? I would have been embarrassed, I suppose, but I'm sure they would have understood the situation.

Situation 4: Another exciting episode occurred when Candice was about two years old. She was speaking in complete sentences by then, and I was bathing her. We were chatting as always. Then, out of the blue, Candice said, "You child abuse me." I was wondering where she had heard such a thing.

Solution: I learned early to always try and stay calm, listen, and gather the facts before reacting. "Candice, how do I child abuse you?" She kept repeating that she was abused. Finally, I said, "Candice, what can I do so you won't feel child abused?" She said, "Take me to the store and buy me whatever I want!"

Rationale: Children learn very early how to manipulate their parents, whether they do it or not. Don't fall into that trap. I informed her she would not get anything, so her tactic did not work. She did not try that again.

Participation

While my two girls were growing up, we were busy with school, work, and activities. I did my best to ensure they could pursue just about anything they wanted. I believed in keeping them engaged because they were less likely to get into trouble. We are all familiar with the saying, "An idle mind is the devil's playground." Exposing them to different activities also helped shape them and identify their goals.

As a result of all their activities, my second job was as a chauffeur. I was always in the car, taking them from one activity to the next, especially on the weekends. I would bring my job-related work to track meets and music lessons so I wouldn't get behind. I sometimes asked the person beside me to let me know when my child was scheduled for her turn. Then, I would put my work down, cheer my girls through their events, and immediately return to it afterward. There was no thinking. I just did it. The important thing was that my children knew I was there for them.

I was always interested in what both my girls were doing. My challenge was balancing being with them and a very demanding job. This was one of the more stressful parts of being a single parent. The piano incident with Danielle paved the way for me to let them participate in any extracurricular activity they mentioned. This included violin lessons, horseback riding, gymnastics, skating, track (sprinting, long jump, hurdles, long distance, high jump), swimming, competitive dance competitions in different states, music recitals, and cheerleading. I also attended Jack and Jill meetings, chaperoned kids of varying age groups, and volunteered on committees. The problem was that I was constantly sleep-deprived, but I kept going.

Whenever I could, I would contact one of their teachers and ask if I could visit the classroom. My daughters were not too happy about this, but it's one of the areas where I made the decision unilaterally. Over time, they got used to it. One time, I visited one of Candice's classes, and it was so out of control that I didn't know how anyone could learn anything. The students were disrespectful to the teacher, talking without permission and out of control. I spoke to Candice about it later when she came home. She did not seem to take issue with it, and I never mentioned it again. She did the required homework and learned the material despite the classroom distractions.

Situation 1: One of my most daring classroom visits was to one of Candice's classes at the University of Southern California Law School. I had asked permission to sit in on the lesson. It just happened that the professor was teaching hospital law, a subject I was very familiar with. He made a statement that was not quite right. What should I do?

Solution: As you may have guessed, I raised my hand! He acknowledged me, and I clarified his previous comments to the class. I looked at Candice; she just looked straight ahead as if I wasn't there.

Rationale: Maybe that was taking things too far, but accuracy is essential to me. Also, I wouldn't want my daughter to wonder why I didn't correct information I knew was not accurate. I tried to do it as unobtrusively as possible to avoid embarrassing Candice, but I'm sure she was not pleased. I thought, what's the point of being involved if I'm not going to contribute when needed?

Situation 2: Danielle had an opportunity to study Spanish in Spain. I encouraged her to go because it would be an excellent experience. She was nineteen years old, and her university had a program for students to attend Santander, in northern Spain, where few tourists went. However, I got concerned about her safety being so far away. What could I do?

Solution: I contacted the university and asked if I could visit my daughter in Spain. They advised against it, which I understood, but as a mother, I decided to go anyway. I had to make sure she was safe. I took time off from work and flew to Madrid. From there, I had to catch a bus for a five-hour ride to Santander. The trip was stressful because I was never sure I was on the right bus. Fortunately, I understood a bit of Spanish. I arrived at the beautiful hotel in a lovely setting but could only think about Danielle. Was she alright?

Once I got to my room, I realized that using the phone would be challenging. I was unsure if I could call Danielle's number because I had to go through the Spanish-speaking operator. Somehow, I got the operator to call the phone number, and Danielle answered the phone! I told her I was in the hotel, which was only a fifteen-minute walk. I was excitedly waiting in the lobby for her and wondering if she was okay.

Danielle walked through the hotel door with the sun shining behind her. She looked beautiful, full of smiles, energy and happiness. I immediately felt at ease. She had the glow of an angel coming down from heaven. All the concern and anxiety lifted from my shoulders. I could finally breathe again. It was like having a meltdown that ended up in joy. I promised that it would not interrupt her classes or homework. Her university told me they did not want her parents to interfere, so I did my best to comply, but I had to ease my mind. We would occasionally get ice cream after her class if she had free time. I was impressed by how she could place the order, speaking only Spanish. I was so proud of her. She was able to take care of herself. I did not have to worry about her anymore. She was enjoying life, and now so was I.

Rationale: I realize that my actions may seem extreme to some, but I learned long ago (and outlined in my plan) that when I was feeling stress or concern impacting other areas of my life, I needed to deal with it. As a mother, I'd do anything to ensure my daughters were as safe as possible, and if that meant flying overseas, so be it. I knew that I had to make sure everything was fine. If I hadn't, I would have continued to be distracted and unfocused while she was gone. It was the best course of action for both of us.

Participation and involvement in children's activities are essential, whether chaperoning a party or traveling around the world. The important thing is that you know what's going on in their lives, no matter what that takes to make that happen.

Parties

Speaking of parties, when my daughters were younger, I would give them birthday parties at home, the after-school program, or Chuck E. Cheese. These events were easy to plan, and it made them feel important. (There were always adults in attendance for supervision if necessary.) This was their day, and all their friends were celebrating with them. Sometimes, I even hired a puppeteer or a clown to entertain. I would always prepare the food and beverages. I made sure they were around children their age with an appropriate number of adults.

My children were amiable and were invited to many parties throughout their school years. One of my requirements for any party they went to was to ensure there would be adult supervision. I would always speak with the parents beforehand to ask if an adult would be present. When I dropped my child off at the house, I would go inside to confirm that a parent was there.

Situation 1: Once, I took Danielle to a house party, and her classmate let us in. I asked where his parents were. He said they had gone to the store.

Solution: I stayed at the party with Danielle until the parents returned. Of course, Danielle was mortified.

Rationale: She laughs about those situations now and understands the importance of ensuring kids are in a safe environment. I never had a problem implementing my plan in those types of situations. I knew she would be embarrassed, but her safety was my top concern.

Situation 2: When Danielle graduated from high school, she informed me that some of her classmates would have an after-party in a hotel room. She wanted to attend.

Solution: I told her she couldn't go and gave her the option of having the after-party at our house. I offered to prepare the food and non-alcoholic beverages, and everyone could spend the night here. She agreed, so some of her friends and their dates came. A few parents felt uncomfortable with the boys and girls sleeping in the same house, but they did not need to have any concerns. To ensure the boys stayed downstairs and the girls upstairs, I slept on the floor by the door, dividing the girls from the boys. There was no way that the door could open without hitting me.

Rationale: My solution may seem extreme, but I can promise you those young people understood the rules and followed them. They were well-behaved, and I enjoyed providing them with a safe environment.

Promises

Teaching children the importance of keeping promises is a fundamental aspect of instilling values such as integrity and trustworthiness in them. Whether the promises are significant or minor, they are critical in establishing one's reliability and are the foundation of trust in any relationship. It's vital for children to learn to honor their commitments, as this helps them comprehend the effects their words and actions have on others. When children grasp the significance of keeping promises, they develop a sense of responsibility and accountability, which in turn earns them the respect and trust of those around them.

Parents can impart this lesson effectively by setting an example. By consistently keeping their promises to their children, parents demonstrate the behavior they expect from their children. Moreover, openly discussing the consequences of not keeping promises and acknowledging the challenges of always being able to fulfill them helps children grasp the complexities surrounding commitments. Such guidance nurtures a sense of moral responsibility and aids in shaping children into dependable and trustworthy adults.

Situation: Danielle had report cards with more B's than A's. One day, I told her that if she brought home a report card with straight A's, she could have all the communication devices available and use them whenever she wanted. (This was similar to providing rewards like my father had done when I started high school.) I knew that these communication privileges were important to her. However, she said she couldn't get all A's.

Solution: Instead of revising my offer, I held firm. I told her I understood, but the privileges I promised would be available if she did. Nothing more was said, and she gave me her report card when the time came. I read it and discovered that she had earned all A's at the end of the following semester! I jumped up from my chair, congratulated her, and took her to the electronics store. She got whatever was available at that time. She was not required to maintain all A's to keep her new privileges. She only wanted to call her friends and classmates. There was no restriction on when she could use the phone. All hours of the day and night were fine with me.

Rationale: I remembered being a teenager and the importance of communicating with my friends; I would hold the telephone receiver under the covers and talk to my boyfriend at night. I heard a news story about parents who would not let their daughters speak on the phone after a specific time. She would sneak out of the house, go to a convenience store, and use the pay phone. One night, she snuck out of her home and was involved in an accident. That story stayed with me, and I had no problem with my children using the phone at any time because I knew they were safe at home. It was vital that they could always count on me to follow through on whatever I said I would say or do. It gives kids a secure feeling of knowing they can depend on you, whether they agree or not.

Safety

As with all parents, safety is always a primary concern. Since this is such an important topic, I want to share a few techniques I used to educate my children while trying to make the lessons interactive and impactful.

Chemicals: My father once shared a tragic story about his younger sister, Violet, who accidentally ingested Lye mixed with a milky substance and passed away. This story deeply impacted me, so when I became a parent, I was determined to educate my children about the potential hazards in a home. I gathered them in front of the closet where all the cleaning and disinfectant bottles were kept. (This was a time before the advent of safety locks on doors and cabinets.) Under my close supervision, I had each child take a bottle and smell its contents. I made sure they experienced the strongest and most unpleasant odors to emphasize my point. I carefully monitored this activity throughout, and as I had hoped, their curiosity was quickly satisfied. They lost interest in the contents of that closet. This exercise effectively curbed their curiosity, and I no longer worried about them accessing the closet again. It also eased my concerns about accidental exposure to chemicals, whether at home or at a friend's house, where such items might not be securely stored.

Nowadays, fortunately, there are child cabinet locks and other safety measures to ensure harmful chemicals are stored safely. However, I believe there are times when unconventional methods, applied safely, are necessary to leave a lasting impression on young minds, teaching them important safety lessons.

Cooking: When it came to the stove, I used one of my mother's lessons. I turned on very low heat and showed them how the burner lit up. Then I would say, "Hot!" and "Burn!" until they understood the importance. I was careful not to let them get too near the heat, but I thought they would not understand fully if I just said it was hot. They needed to feel the warmth for themselves, from a safe distance, of course.

Sports: Since the girls were involved in various activities, I made it a point never to label their clothes or equipment with their names. I also ensured that if I could not transport them, I was informed of when they reached their destination.

Strangers: Every day on the way to school. I would ask them what they would say if a stranger approached them and offered them candy to go with them. They were to shout, "NO!" What if the stranger says your mother is sick, in the hospital, and calling for you? They were to shout, "NO!" They were taught that if I sent a stranger to inform them to go with them, that person would know the secret word. I told them if I could not send someone with a secret word, they knew who to contact and have that trusted friend find out if I was okay. We practiced that all the time.

Swimming: Another aspect of their development I identified as necessary was swimming. I wanted my children to learn how to be safe in the water, so I consciously committed myself to doing everything I could to make the learning activity fun for each of them. Candice was enrolled in classes when she was eighteen months old. She was unafraid of the water and learned to swim quickly. My only involvement was providing the opportunity for lessons and supervising her progress.

Danielle was different. She had a fear of the water. When I would take her swimming, she would scream and panic. Danielle was so afraid of the water that she would only get in the pool if I joined her. She would cling to me for dear life. That was fine. I just had to ensure I had time to spend with her until she felt more comfortable.

Weather: When Candice and Danielle were born, we lived in Michigan. The weather could be frigid in the winter. There were news stories of children waking up early, opening the front or back door, and venturing outside only to freeze to death in the winter. During cold weather, I was always on alert.

Self-Control (Parent and Child)

When Danielle was a young teenager, she often kept her room in a disheveled state. I had an expectation that both of my daughters would maintain their rooms in a reasonably tidy manner. Danielle frequently had friends over, and they would spend time in her cluttered bedroom. Despite my repeated requests for her to clean it up, she didn't comply. One day, she emerged from her room and declared in a very mature tone, "Mom, I am not going to clean my room." I listened calmly as she presented her reasoning. She admitted that she hadn't been cleaning it and probably never would. I appreciated her honesty (as per our house rule, which states there's no punishment for telling the truth) and then requested that she avoid bringing food into her room and keep the door closed.

We reached a compromise, which brought peace to our household. I agreed to her terms, and life became simpler for both of us. Interestingly, as an adult, Danielle has become extremely tidy. Guests must remove their shoes upon entering her home, dishes must be washed immediately after meals, and her closets must be impeccably organized. When she visits me, she even cleans out my refrigerator and kitchen cabinets. This transformation amazed me and taught me that children can change as they mature. I'm glad I allowed her to make her own decision about her room. Perhaps the extremity of her messiness led her to resolve never to live in such disarray again. Had I forced her to clean every day, she might have developed a subconscious desire to maintain a messy home as an adult. I also wanted to avoid daily arguments about her room, as that wasn't the kind of relationship that I wished to have with her or Candice.

Situation 1: When we first moved to Georgia, Candice was in after-school childcare, where a boy called her the N-word.
Solution: The teacher told me that Candice didn't get upset. She walked over to the dictionary, looked up the word, and showed the boy saying, "This word describes you more than it does me." I asked the teacher if I should talk to the parents of the boy, but she said, "No, Candice took care of it."
Rationale: I have also always told them that if anything negative happens, we will follow three steps. One, tell me about it. Two, I will discuss it with you. Three, I will not take any action without their permission. That was important to me because if they knew that I wouldn't overreact, they could confide in me (at least until they were teenagers). I think about that moment often because it showed me that they were learning the lessons I'd hoped they would.

Situation 2: I was involved in a lawsuit and hired an attorney who was out of state. I was displeased with the lack of communication from this attorney. I needed more contact than I was getting. With Candice being a lawyer, I was complaining about my displeasure. This was not acceptable. I was paying this attorney, and I deserved to be treated better. I was complaining and whining. I wanted her to advise me on how to get my attorney to meet my expectations. She finally told me that the cases she was assigned did not require the communication that I expected. In other words, I was not the type of person she was used to working with and could not help me.

Solution: I used a lot of self-control. I had to bite my tongue many times! According to my parenting plan, I would not allow myself to get upset over something I could not control.

Rationale: I had to ignore it. I told myself that she did not want to get involved and had no advice for me. I had taught her to speak up and tell me whatever was on her mind. As a parent, remember to stick to your PPP even when times get tough!

Situation 3: Candice, her husband, and her baby visited me in Michigan. This was the second time I had seen my granddaughter, Jordyn. Candice wanted to leave Jordyn with me while she and her husband went to dinner. I was thrilled. However, before I could babysit, Candice said she had to interview me! That caught me off guard, but I agreed. We were sitting across from each other at the kitchen table, and she interviewed me like I was applying for a real nanny job. She asked questions like a prosecuting attorney, and I was on the witness stand. It felt like I was being treated like I was guilty of some horrible crime. One question I remember had to do with warming breast milk. She must have wanted to ensure I would not use the microwave and that I would heat the milk in a pot just like "in the olden days." It felt like an interrogation and was somewhat uncomfortable; I was very annoyed, but I did answer all of her questions. She asked many questions trying to confirm to herself that I was competent enough to take care of her daughter.

Solution: At the end of the interview, she said I had passed, but I didn't feel victorious. I felt disrespected and a bit insulted. I stayed calm because I had to allow her to manage her child's care independently. However, I did have to speak my mind. I thanked her for permitting me to take care of my granddaughter. I also reminded her, "I do have experience taking care of children. Remember, I am your mother and took reasonably good care of you, don't you agree?" She thought about what I said and then did not verbally agree!

Rationale: It took Herculean self-control not to jump across the table! All the years of planning and trying to do my best, and that was the gratitude I got! These are the times when self-control is crucial! I also had to remind myself that her focus was caring for her child, and, like her mother, she wanted things done a certain way. That meant no one was immune to her inquisitions, not even me!

Situation 4: At one of my jobs, our department was having difficulty making decisions, and it was affecting our performance. I was frustrated with the situation.

Solution: Our employer hired a mental health expert who helped us understand why we were having difficulties. It was because we were acting out our own fixations of childhood. We learned it is essential to be aware of our behaviors and ensure we are not acting out based on childhood frustrations.

Rationale: When it comes to self-control, parents need to understand where their own internalized feelings come from because that will help them better understand their children's feelings.

Self-Esteem

Building self-esteem in children is crucial to their emotional and psychological development, laying the foundation for their future confidence and self-worth. It involves creating an environment where children feel valued, capable, and accepted for who they are. This process begins with positive reinforcement, praising achievements, effort, resilience, and the courage to try new things. It's important to encourage children to embrace their unique qualities and to understand that mistakes are a natural part of learning and growth. Parents and caregivers should model self-esteem by treating themselves and others respectfully and kindly, as children often mirror adult behaviors.

Setting realistic expectations and providing consistent, unconditional support contribute significantly to a child's self-esteem. Involving children in decision-making and listening to their opinions fosters a sense of empowerment and belonging. By nurturing these aspects, children develop a strong self-esteem, which is instrumental in navigating life's challenges with confidence and optimism.

Situation: I was focused on building self-esteem in each daughter. I wanted to negate as much negativity as possible.

Solution: My approach was to be direct. I told my children that our ancestors came from Africa, the birthplace of civilization. I constantly reminded them they were descendants of kings and queens. I firmly believe that they should know themselves and not let anyone try to define them.

Rationale: I strived to increase their self-esteem in any way I could. Whether it was a big event or something minor, I always looked for opportunities to tell them how important they were and that no one could change that.

Sibling Rivalry

Sibling rivalry is inevitable, so managing its impact on your family is important. Firstly, unchecked rivalry can escalate into persistent conflicts, eroding the foundation of trust and companionship that siblings should ideally share. Such continuous discord not only affects the immediate family atmosphere, making it stressful and tense but also impacts the emotional and psychological well-being of the children involved. When children constantly compete or fight, they may develop self-esteem insecurity issues and struggle with establishing healthy relationships outside the family.

Furthermore, sibling rivalry can divert attention from individual needs and strengths, as children may focus more on outdoing one another rather than fostering their unique talents. Managing and controlling these rivalries ensures a more harmonious home environment and helps nurture confident, emotionally balanced individuals who value relationships and understand the essence of teamwork and collaboration.

Situation 1: Candice was my first child, so I had some concerns when I became pregnant with Danielle. I didn't want her to feel like she had been replaced or was no longer special to me.

Solution: I involved her in the experience by telling her she would have a little sister or brother. We would discuss the impending birth and how she would be elevated to the role of a big sister! I told Candice how exciting it would be for her since she was knowledgeable and could teach the new baby so much.

When Danielle was born, I had my husband go to the childcare center and bring Candice to the hospital to see her new sister. When Candice arrived, she was placed on a chair that we called a "pedestal" to view her new sister. The first thing Candice said was, "Where is the ice cream and cake? This is Danielle's birthday, and you are supposed to have ice cream and cake!" The nurse immediately left the room and brought back the treats.

Rationale: Candice felt heard, and her importance in the family dynamic was established early on.

Situation 2: When I brought Danielle home, my closest friends wanted to meet the new baby, but I was concerned about all the attention placed solely on the baby. I didn't want Candice to feel left out.

Solution: I welcomed anyone who wanted to visit to drop by, but I also asked them not to bring gifts unless they brought two, one for Candice and one for Danielle. Secondly, I asked them not to look at the new baby right away. All my friends were in the living room, just having casual discussions. Finally, Candice said, "Don't you want to see my little sister?" Of course, they all said sure and thanked Candice for her suggestion. I placed Danielle in Candice's lap while she sat on the couch. I made sure she was not going to be dropped. Candice did all the talking and explained what we had to do, how the baby cried, and how helpful she was in caring for the baby.

Rationale: Following my plan helped remind me not to let the excitement of the blessed event eclipse the importance and significance of my other daughter. That's why it's important to evaluate your PPP's effectiveness constantly. Candice's reactions and behaviors confirmed that my plan was working. She could articulate what she had been told and how she had been treated. Now, she was instructing Danielle using the objectives from the plan as it had been implemented for her. It was a joy to see. There was confirmation that she had listened to what she had been taught and now had the critical job of teaching her little sister. It was wonderful.

Situation 3: There were times when Candice would get frustrated or annoyed with her little sister and try to hit her. Sometimes, I'd catch her hand just before it landed on Danielle.

Solution: I never meted out any punishment for that. I would explain to Candice that she was not allowed to hit her little sister, and Danielle would grow out of whatever was annoying her. When Candice did something positive as it related to Danielle, she was rewarded royally. In time, the positive reinforcement of desirable behavior became the norm. Candice became protective of her little sister as the years went by. Even as a teenager, Candice would have behaviors that annoyed Danielle. I would tell Danielle that Candice would grow out of it!

Rationale: Reacting on impulse can often exacerbate the situation. It's not always easy, but try to stop and communicate with your child in a rational manner. Avoid being judgmental or dismissive.

Address sibling rivalry from the very beginning. Most firstborn children have difficulty adjusting to a new sibling. It is natural for a child getting all the attention to be upset about getting less attention. As we all know, a new baby requires much time and care. It is easy to understand why an older sibling might feel jealous. I gave much thought to how I would handle sibling rivalry. The first step is to be aware that it exists and not just assume it will work itself out. Give the older children individual attention so they feel as important as that newborn everyone fusses over. If you handle it carefully, they will learn that they are equally valued and essential in their own way.

Spouse/Partner

For a single parent, venturing into the world of dating or considering remarriage can significantly impact children. This transition often brings about a range of emotions and adjustments for the children involved. Parents need to approach this change with sensitivity and open communication. Children may experience feelings of uncertainty, jealousy, or fear of being displaced or losing the exclusive attention of their parents.

On the other hand, introducing a new partner can also bring positive dynamics, such as additional love, support, and stability, into the family structure. The parent must reassure their children of their unchanging love and priority while gradually and thoughtfully integrating the new partner into the family dynamic. This process requires patience, understanding, and, often, time for the children to adapt and build trust.

In the best scenarios, the new relationship can offer children the experience of healthy, loving partnerships and enrich their family life. However, it is always important to prioritize the emotional well-being and security of the children in these situations. With a robust PPP, you can thoughtfully plan for and manage these events.

Situation: I was fortunate to have practiced as a Psychiatric Social Worker at the Watts Health Center after graduating. I loved that job. In addition, I studied and met the requirements to be a marriage counselor. One of the lessons I learned is that when you remarry with young children, they are often not thrilled about it.

Solution: While I knew that getting married again was an option, being well aware of how that can impact children, I decided to put that on hold. I decided that I would not remarry while they were small. Even dating was kept to a minimum because I did not have the energy to deal with it, and it was not a priority. At some point, it would be, but not at that time. The children needed my undivided attention since I was filling the role of two parents when they were with me.

Rationale: Having men in the house was not something that I was going to allow. I knew that could cause confusion. When talking with my friends, I emphatically stated that I didn't want to be set up on dates and that I might never get married again. I knew that marriage required a lot of hard work, and I already had my hands full just caring for my two girls and my job.

When the girls finished college and were living in Texas and California, I found love again. Even though my girls were adults, there was still some concern on their part about what I was doing. (Remember, the PPP is not just for raising young children but applies to adult children.)

Both of my girls gave me their input. Danielle said, "Why are you seeing this man?" Candice added, "Mom, you don't know anything about men!" My future husband had a grown son and daughter, so I'm sure his children were wondering about me as well. Did I have an ulterior motive?

One of the first times my fiancé, Chris, was in the car with the three of us, he was driving, and I was in the front passenger seat. Candice was in the back seat, sitting behind Chris. Danielle was sitting behind me. Candice has never been shy about speaking up. After all, she was a lawyer looking out for her mother! She began the discussion by asking if the relationship with her mother was a "rebound situation!" She was in full lawyer mode. (Chris' first wife had passed away about two years before that.)

I just froze and continued looking straight ahead. Sometimes, according to your PPP, it's best to wait before speaking, so that's what I did. Chris did a great job of staying calm and answering her questions. He said that he loved his first wife, who was now gone, and he loved me. And in summary, his intentions were honorable. Apparently, what he said satisfied her, and we all finally relaxed.

Today, Chris considers both my girls as his daughters. Their relationship has blossomed over the seventeen years we have been married. Chris' son and daughter are my son and daughter. Everyone was an adult and living in different homes when we got married, so we avoided some of the pitfalls of a second marriage that can occur with young children being in the house. Interestingly, even though our children were adults, they still had serious concerns about Chris and me getting married! Accepting their parents in a new relationship will probably be difficult regardless of the children's age, but it's all in how it's handled.

Teaching

One of my skills and strengths is observing and listening to others. Watching their behavior and listening to the impact of their behavior has been a practical learning tool. I watched other parents tell their kids, "Don't do that," "Don't touch that," "Don't say that," and "Don't take drugs." Most of us have witnessed telling a child not to do something, which is the first thing they want to do. This happened when Candice was about four years old.

Situation 1: We went to Chuck E. Cheese and ordered pizza. When the food arrived, the waiter said, "Don't touch it; it's hot." I echoed the sentiment. What did Candice do? She reached out and touched the pizza. Fortunately, she did not hurt herself.

Solution: This occurred after I had instructed them about heat and safety. The lesson here is that repetition is key. Education requires repetition and reinforcement. When teaching moments presented themselves, I would ask the girls what they thought, and I would let them think about it.

One of the ways I educated my girls was while watching TV together. When we had time to watch a show, I tried to steer the children to programs that allowed me to instruct them on acceptable and unacceptable behaviors. I remember watching a Western. The storyline was about someone who lied and got caught and how life was worse for him. If he had told the truth from the beginning, none of the bad outcomes he faced would have occurred.

This gave me a chance to teach without feeling forced or planned. I would say, "Look what happened to the man who did not tell the truth. What do you think of that? Life would have been much better if he had only been honest." My kids already knew there was no punishment for telling the truth, and I took every opportunity to reinforce that.

Another movie we watched was about a man telling women how much he loved them, though he never intended to marry them. He would love them and leave them broken-hearted. I pointed out that behavior to my girls using the movie characters as examples.

Rationale: I followed the adage that it's better to show, not just tell. I made it a point to refrain from telling my children specifically what to do and what not to do. Instead, I chose to highlight examples as they occurred.

Situation 2: While Candice was attending college, I wanted Danielle to get excited about higher education and understand the responsibilities and rewards ahead of her.

Solution: I talked to Danielle about the advantages of going to college and the fun I had in school. I also stressed the importance of making intelligent choices and maximizing the opportunity. When I was with my old college friends, we would always talk and laugh about our experiences, and Danielle would be present, watching and listening. We would always stress the social life, the parties, and all the fun we had in college. I very seldom spoke of the studying and the classes.

Rationale: Who wants to know about the hours spent in the library and the difficult tests you studied for all night? To prepare Danielle, I arranged for her to visit Candice at college on a weekend when there would be many parties and lots of socializing. Danielle may have been fifteen or sixteen, old enough to fly alone.

That weekend, Candice was very protective and ensured Danielle was well supervised. Danielle had a wonderful time, further reinforcing her desire to go to college without me having to convince her. Candice admitted to me later that she watched over Danielle using many of my techniques.

Time

As a single parent, my most significant enemy was "time," not enough of it. No matter what needed to be done, there were only twenty-four hours each day. It was like a brick wall that I ran into constantly. My job was challenging, and I even had to carry a beeper that could go off at any time, day or night, weekday or weekend. The balancing act between being with my children, managing the household, and meeting the responsibilities of my job was daunting. Sometimes, I needed to be in two places at the same time. Thus, I relied heavily on my parenting plan to help me handle my responsibilities with minimal stress.

Situation: One of the times I was anxious involved my two girls in recitals and plays. Candice was playing the violin in downtown Atlanta. Danielle had a solo at school in Marietta, GA. Both of these events were scheduled at the same time. Everyone knows about the traffic in Atlanta. How was I going to see Candice and Danielle perform?

Solution: I went into solution mode and treated the situation like a work issue. I got copies of the programs for both events. I studied them and determined at what time each would be performing. With some luck, I could see them both based on where their solo or concert was on the program. I dropped Danielle off at her school early. I then drove Candice downtown, and since her performance was sooner, I stayed and listened to her. As soon as that was over, I faced the daunting traffic and arrived at Danielle's school in Marietta, GA, in time to see her perform. Then I had to drive back to downtown Atlanta, pick up Candice, return to Danielle's school, and take them home.

Rationale: To this day, I don't know how I did it, but I'm glad I did! There was some luck involved. The lesson is don't give up, no matter how difficult the challenge you are facing. As a result, I do believe you will be able to be more successful in overcoming adverse situations.

As my plan outlined, I adopted some small behaviors and time-saving ways to maximize my time. For example:

- I prioritized going to warehouse clubs and buying as much in bulk as possible. The last thing I wanted to do was to have to take the children to the store during the week. Buying in bulk also meant fewer shopping trips and more time for other activities. It was also cost-effective.
- I only bought clothes that were machine washable. I did not have time to go to the dry cleaners. I made sure my washer and dryer were in good condition.
- One chore I had at home was to put clean sheets on the bed and have clean towels for the children. The towels were easy. Mak-

ing up the beds was more time-consuming, but I felt it was an important example to set.
- Since I was single and sleeping on a queen-sized bed, I would only use one-third of the bed each week. That meant I only had to change my sheets once every three weeks. I continued to change the children's sheet once a week or more often if I needed to.
- When the two girls were at the toddler stage or a little older but still needed supervision, I needed to be up at six a.m. every morning. They woke up early but had been taught not to get out of bed without asking permission first. That was the decision I had made for their safety. That meant I had to acknowledge them so they could start the day.
- After the children were asleep on Friday night, I would shower, sleep in a sweat suit (hoping it would not get too wrinkled!) and be ready the next day. That saved some time in the mornings and allowed me to get them dressed and fed promptly.

These examples of what I did won't suit every situation. Identify actions that you can take to save time and do them. Also, incorporate them into your PPP so that you'll have it documented, which will soon become second nature.

Candice playing the violin

8

Collect Feedback

For me, the fourth and final phase of the Purposeful Parenting Plan, gathering feedback, turned out to be an enlightening experience. As my children matured, I recognized the importance of understanding their views on their upbringing. I was curious about which aspects they found helpful and which they did not. I also wanted to know whether they felt well-prepared for life's challenges. To explore these questions, I arranged several Zoom meetings with them since they now live in different states. This approach was consistent with a fundamental principle of the PPP: involving the children in decisions and valuing their perspectives. Even as adults, their insights on the effectiveness of a parenting plan can be invaluable.

These discussions, filled with laughter and reminiscence, provided a platform for candid feedback from their point of view. My educational background taught me the importance of evaluating hypotheses; in this case, the parenting plan was my subject. It was rewarding to learn that the outcomes of my parenting were apparent in their adult lives. Their perspectives were fascinating and enlightening.

I approached their feedback with an open mind, ready to accept their thoughts without guilt, and confident in my parenting efforts. My daughters were honest and acknowledged my parenting style and how they adapted. Through our conversations, I learned that certain events were more memorable to one than the other, highlighting our perceptions of significance, but I wanted to know more. I delved deeper into their thoughts on my approach to parenting.

Certainly, their professional achievements filled me with immense pride. Now a senior legal counsel, Candice passed the California Bar exam on her first try at age twenty-four. Danielle had earned her master's degree in Human Dimensions of Organizations, successfully applying her knowledge as Sr. Vice President in a school district. They credited my parenting approach with giving them the motivation to aim high and the tools to handle adversity. They appreciated the values instilled in them, such as physical fitness, healthy eating, adequate sleep, and community service.

They grew up confident in expressing their opinions, knowing they wouldn't be punished for their words or actions. They understood my strictness and desire for control, particularly in their younger years, but also recognized how they longed for more freedom. They humorously remembered my cautious approach to their outings, including when I took them to a movie, realized it was rated "R," and promptly turned around and took them back home – a moment I had forgotten!

Candice shared her comfort in diverse social settings, attributing that skill to her upbringing, and Danielle echoed the sentiment, feeling at ease in varied social circles. Both daughters exhibit high self-esteem and have integrated my teachings into their lives, including showing respect for all, regardless of socioeconomic status.

Candice often recalled my guidance during challenging parenting moments with her daughter, while Danielle found herself applying my advice in various life situations. Their continued reliance on my counsel affirmed the lasting impact of my parenting style.

In one memorable conversation, Danielle referred to my style as "Gentle Parenting," a term new to me. After researching, I found it emphasized respect, empathy, understanding, and boundaries – principles that aligned with my approach. She highlighted children's adaptability, resilience, and forgiving nature and that mistakes are a natural part of parenting. The absence of trauma in their upbringing and the positive environment they were raised in were points of gratitude for her. These heartening conversations with my daughters reinforced the success of my parenting approach and its positive influence on their lives.

Impostor Syndrome

One day, Danielle called to discuss "Impostor Syndrome." Despite evidence of success, she described it as a persistent feeling of inadequacy. Those affected often doubt their accomplishments and fear being exposed as a fraud, even when competently fulfilling their roles.

Danielle wondered how I raised her and her sister without them developing this perceived inadequacy. As I contemplated her question, she shared her perspective, crediting the varied experiences of their childhood. She fondly recalled our Christmas dinners at the Ritz-Carlton and other diverse settings, which she believed bolstered her confidence and comfort in any environment.

This conversation led me to reflect on the early development of behaviors associated with Impostor Syndrome. I remember encouraging Danielle to embrace challenges, even when she hesitated due to fear or uncertainty. For instance, I nudged her to make her appointments, like booking a hair salon visit, which initially intimidated her. Gradually, she grew comfortable with such tasks.

Another example was when Danielle moved to Houston for a job with Teach for America, feeling nervous about relocating alone. I encouraged her to navigate this independently, offering support and advice remotely. I helped her with house hunting in Houston but emphasized the importance of her taking the lead.

Candice also experienced self-doubt, especially during her transition from middle to high school. On her first day, she expressed worries about being accepted by her new peers. I reassured her of her charming personality and past friendships, confidently dispelling any unwarranted fears about fitting in at high school.

These instances highlighted the value of cultivating self-confidence and independence in my children. They learned to trust their abilities and judgment by confronting and surmounting small challenges. This approach effectively protected them from Impostor Syndrome, equipping them to approach life confidently and resiliently. Danielle's reflections affirmed the success of my parenting approach, which emphasized facing fears, fostering self-reliance, and instilling a strong sense of self-worth.

Give Yourself Feedback...and Grace.

Undertaking a personal evaluation based on the myriad experiences encountered while raising children is an integral aspect of parenting. This process involves keenly observing them across various situations, carefully noting how they adapt and respond to diverse life experiences. This observation allows parents to gauge the effectiveness of their PPP.

Several criteria can be used to measure this success:

- Have the children chosen careers that align with their passions?
- Do they exhibit argumentative behavior toward family members and peers or engage constructively?
- Are they deriving enjoyment from life?
- Do they exhibit traits of happiness and good citizenship?
- And, importantly, have the goals set out in the PPP been realized?

Over the years, as my children grew, I consistently assessed the success of my parenting strategy. This plan wasn't rigid; it evolved and adapted based on new situations we encountered. My nature of diligently following through was vital in this ongoing process. Daily feedback came in many forms: through observing their behavior, celebrating their achievements, and watching their interactions with peers in social settings, where they consistently seemed to integrate seamlessly.

A critical component of their upbringing was teaching my daughters to be independent and confidently voice their needs and desires. Given the nature of my job, which often required me to be away from home, I knew the importance of them being able to stand on their own. This also included learning to be assertive when necessary.

In her childhood, Danielle wasn't naturally inclined to assertiveness, particularly with adults. It wasn't about being confrontational but ensuring she could ask questions and safeguard her interests without feeling intimidated. Recognizing this, I consciously decided to nurture this skill in her. She needed to handle such situations herself rather than deferring to me. Ultimately, both daughters learned this lesson in self-advocacy well. They now even assist me in maintaining assertiveness in my dealings, demonstrating their comfort in interacting confidently with people of all ages, backgrounds, and social classes.

A memorable moment was when Danielle graduated college with her bachelor's degree and planned her move to Houston. I encouraged her to embark on homeownership, offering my assistance. She adeptly selected potential homes, showcasing her ability to prioritize and manage her finances, skills we had developed together over the years. Our trip to Houston to finalize her home purchase was a testament to her growing independence and decision-making skills.

I was prepared to offer financial assistance during the home purchasing process, even considering co-signing her mortgage loan. Despite having no tangible assets or savings and having just completed her education, Danielle managed to secure the loan independently, much to my astonishment. Her creditworthiness exceeded mine, enabling her to obtain the loan without a deposit and without my financial backing. This marked a significant milestone, evidence of her growth, independence, and the success of the plan. Her playful teasing about this situation only underscored her newfound confidence and autonomy.

Danielle's teaching career further illustrated the positive outcomes of her upbringing. When I visited her classroom, I was profoundly impressed by her teaching prowess. She effectively motivated her students, resulting in a remarkable 90% improvement in their test scores within her first year of teaching. Her control over the classroom and her ability to impart practical learning skills were evident. Her success led to several well-deserved promotions, and she now holds an influential role in administration, advising principals and teachers. We had carefully weighed the pros and cons of a teaching career, but her decision to follow her heart into this profession brought her immense satisfaction and happiness.

Candice, who displays exceptional talent both as an athlete and a musician and consistently excels academically, had many career options. She could have chosen many different career paths and would have been successful. Her career aspirations became apparent at the age of eleven during a television interview on "Talk of the Town," where she confidently stated her ambition to become a lawyer. Pursuing this goal, she graduated from law school at the University of Southern California and successfully passed a notably challenging bar exam. The qualities that define a successful lawyer – astute debating skills, organized thought processes, and persuasive abilities – have been evident in Candice from a very young age.

I recall a particular instance when Candice was only three years old. After a shopping trip, she persuasively argued for us to have lunch at the mall, presenting well-reasoned arguments demonstrating her innate talent for logical reasoning and persuasion. Despite deciding against her suggestion, I was struck by her ability to articulate her thoughts clearly and persuasively. This early display of talent foreshadowed her successful pursuit of a legal career.

The journey of parenting, guided by the plan, has been profoundly fulfilling and successful. Observing my daughters develop into independent, confident, and successful adults has been a profound testament to the effectiveness of my parenting strategies. Their achievements in their respective careers and overall happiness and contentment are sources of immense pride and joy.

The Grandkids and Their Point of View

Recently, I seized a chance to talk with my four grandchildren about how they perceive me as a grandparent. Candice has two children, and Ayanna, my husband's daughter, whom I equally cherish as my own, also has two children. During our talk, one of Ayanna's sons offered his perspective, describing me as kind and generous, radiating a generally positive spirit. He observed that I tend to be exceptionally organized and often have a specific way I like things done, which can sometimes be a bit "pushy and demanding."

He confessed that there are moments when he feels a bit uneasy, particularly when I encourage him to engage in activities that he is less inclined toward, like being more assertive, taking risks, and working on his weaknesses. Interestingly, he pointed out that I might sometimes be a bit unfair to his grandfather, my husband, which made me humorously think about how the males in our family often seem to band together! However, he perceived my treatment of others as positive and expressed his hope for my happiness.

This conversation was quite revealing, especially since I rarely see my grandchildren, given they all reside in different states. His reflections made me realize he hadn't consistently experienced my parenting approach as I applied my plan guidelines. This has been a gentle reminder for me to be more conscious of not being too assertive or "pushy," particularly in my interactions with grandchildren whose mother I didn't raise. This experience has been enlightening and offers valuable lessons for parents who remarry and blend new children into their families. It underscores the significance of thoughtfully navigating these new relationships and tailoring one's approach to the unique dynamics of a blended family.

My great grandmother, Nealy Beal Douglas, my grandmother, Birdie Beal Anderson

9

The Evolution of Parenting Styles

To fully appreciate how my parenting style compares and contrasts with that of my parents and to understand its impact on my daughters and grandchildren, it's essential to first consider the broader evolution of parenting over the past fifty years or so. My research indicates that parenting approaches have undergone remarkable changes during this time, reflecting broader shifts in societal values, cultural norms, and advancements in our understanding of psychology. Understanding these changes, along with their benefits and limitations, is crucial for recognizing the context and implications of these shifts in the realm of contemporary parenting. This awareness helps navigate the nuances of modern parenting strategies, offering a rich perspective on how these generational differences in parenting styles shape family dynamics and individual growth.

Authoritarian to More Flexible Approaches

During the 1960s and 1970s, the dominant parenting style was essentially authoritarian, characterized by a strong emphasis on strict discipline, respect for authority, and obedience, all grounded in traditional values. However, as these decades unfolded, mainly influenced by the cultural revolutions of the 1960s, there was a noticeable trend toward more permissive and democratic parenting styles. These emerging approaches placed a higher value on open communication, emotional expression, and fostering children's individuality. A significant positive outcome of this evolution in parenting was an increased recognition of children's emotional needs.

Nevertheless, this shift also presented challenges, notably in some households, with a noticeable decrease in discipline and structure. This period marked a crucial transition in parenting philosophies, balancing the need for structure with a deeper understanding of children's emotional and individual development.

The Rise of Authoritative Parenting

In the 1980s and 1990s, authoritative parenting emerged as a popular style, bridging the gap between the earlier authoritarian and permissive extremes. This approach was marked by firm yet fair discipline, setting high expectations while providing support and warmth. It emphasized nurturing a child's independence and self-esteem. This period has significantly contributed to parenting practices by recognizing the importance of balancing structure with emotional support, which is vital for fostering healthy psychological development in children.

However, one challenge during this era was the increasing pressure on parents to achieve "perfection," which sometimes led to unrealistic expectations and stress. Despite this, the era represents a pivotal shift toward a more holistic understanding of children's needs, paving the way for more balanced and supportive parenting approaches.

The Helicopter and Lawnmower Trends

At the turn of the century, new parenting trends, such as helicopter parenting and lawnmower parenting, began to gain traction. These styles are characterized by high overprotectiveness and involvement in children's lives, where parents actively work to eliminate obstacles and challenges that their children might face. Stemming from a well-intentioned desire to ensure the best for their children, these methods often led to unintended consequences, such as diminished resilience and independence among young people.

While the primary goal of these approaches was to secure children's success and well-being, they sometimes resulted in young adults facing difficulties in problem-solving and emotional coping. Despite these challenges, these trends highlight the evolving nature of parenting, reflecting a deep-seated commitment to nurturing and protecting children, albeit with a recognition of the need for balance in fostering children's autonomy and resilience.

Emphasis on Emotional Intelligence and Mindful Parenting

In recent times, parenting styles have further evolved to emphasize emotional intelligence, mindfulness, and a partnership-oriented approach between parents and children. This contemporary shift underscores the significance of understanding and effectively managing emotions in parents and children. It advocates for a collaborative relationship grounded in dialogue, mutual respect, and understanding. This approach aims to promote emotional health and resilience in children.

However, it also presents the challenge of striking a balance between empathy and the necessary boundaries and discipline. This evolution in parenting demonstrates a progressive understanding of child development, focusing on nurturing emotionally intelligent and resilient individuals while maintaining a healthy structure in the family dynamic.

The Digital Age Impact

The advent of the digital age has notably reshaped parenting, bringing unique challenges such as overseeing screen time, ensuring online safety, and addressing the effects of social media on children's self-esteem and perspectives on the world. In this era, parents have found themselves adapting to dual roles: as guides in both the tangible, physical world and the expansive, virtual realm. This transition highlights the evolving nature of parenting in a technology-driven world, emphasizing the importance of equipping children with the skills to navigate digital and physical spaces safely and responsibly.

A Journey of Adaptation and Learning

The parenting journey has been a testament to continuous adaptation to evolving societal dynamics and an expanding understanding of child psychology. Each historical period has contributed valuable insights while presenting its unique challenges. Today's parents benefit from this rich historical tapestry of parenting styles. They can blend the structure and discipline characteristic of earlier times with the emotional awareness and adaptability that have come to the fore in more recent trends.

The crucial aspect lies in striking a harmonious balance that caters to the distinct needs of each child and family. This approach ensures that the progressive evolution of parenting styles remains supportive and conducive to children's healthy development in a rapidly changing world.

My mother, Vora Thompson Wilson, and my father, Charles Stanley Wilson, Sr. on their wedding day

10

Generational Parenting Styles

Delving into the evolution of parenting styles has significantly enhanced my understanding of my own experiences and journey. Reflecting on my family's rich history, which spans from my childhood through my years as a mother and now in my role as a grandmother, I can see the distinct progression of these styles. Each generation within our family has brought its unique approach to parenting, drawing from the wisdom of the past and, in turn, shaping the future of our family's parenting traditions.

In my childhood, my parents' approach was firmly rooted in stability and survival, with a strong focus on providing the necessary resources for us to thrive. Our household was characterized by firm discipline and high expectations, with emotional expression being less common. My parents were incredibly hard-working, with limited leisure time. My mother, the heart of our home, ensured we were well-fed, and our clothes were always neat and clean. As the primary breadwinner, my father expressed his love through his relentless work ethic, dedicating countless hours to ensure we were well provided. Our family interactions were primarily practical, centered around chores, academic responsibilities, and an unquestionable respect for elders.

When I transitioned into parenthood, the world was undergoing significant changes. Influenced by the Civil Rights movement, women's liberation, and evolving socio-cultural values, my approach to parenting was markedly different. I was committed to ensuring that my children felt cared for, valued, and understood. While I maintained the discipline and structure instilled by my parents, I fostered an environment rich in open discussions, encouraging debates, dreams, and even healthy defiance at times.

Aiming for a harmonious balance, I sought to instill in my children the resilience and work ethic I had learned from my upbringing. Simultaneously, I encouraged them to challenge norms, be inquisitive, and express themselves openly. As a single mother, navigating this fusion of traditional and contemporary approaches often felt like venturing into uncharted territory, filled with moments of uncertainty and reflection on whether this blend would sufficiently prepare them for the future.

Watching my daughter, Candice, navigate parenting in the digital age has been an enlightening and humbling experience. Her approach is infused with mindfulness and a focus on open dialogues about emotions, emphasizing the importance of individuality in her children. She adopts a collaborative parenting style, making decisions as a family unit with adaptable boundaries to each child's specific needs. Despite the ubiquitous presence of technology, she remains conscious of its use, ensuring it acts as a tool for growth and learning.

What is particularly striking in her approach is the emphasis on mental well-being. She is acutely aware of her children's emotional needs, fostering a strong sense of self-worth, resilience, and adaptability in them.

Exploring diverse parenting styles across generations within our family has been a profoundly insightful journey. It highlights the similarities and differences that weave through our family's narrative. Reflecting on the evolution of parenting within our family provides a valuable perspective, offering insights that might resonate with your family's journey and shed light on the ongoing transformation of parenting practices across generations.

My Parents

Reflecting on the formative years of my upbringing, I am profoundly aware of the fortunate circumstances I was born into, having parents who were not only educated but also holders of postgraduate degrees. My mother was in her late twenties, and my father was in his late thirties at my birth. They had both fully experienced life as singles and as a married couple before they embarked on the journey of parenthood. This maturity and their established careers contributed significantly to the stability and structured environment that characterized my early life.

My father, the second youngest in a large family of thirteen children, and my mother, who grew up as an only child, brought a unique blend of discipline and nurturing to their parenting styles. Notably, they chose to refrain from physical punishment, partly influenced by my natural tendency to adhere to rules and avoid trouble. Our home was a haven of consistency, with well-established routines that provided a deep sense of security and predictability. They instilled in me the importance of rest, the value of healthy eating, and the necessity of maintaining a well-rounded life, balancing time between church, school, and a vibrant social life. Throughout my childhood, I felt an overwhelming sense of being loved and supported, yet my parents were careful not to be overbearing or to hover over me.

My father's role as a teacher brought unique skills into our home, particularly in understanding and motivating teenagers. His background in a large family and his professional experience gave him keen insights into children's behavior and communication styles. His easygoing demeanor made him a delightful presence in our lives. When he was off from teaching, our summers were filled with playful activities and laughter. His gentle guidance, often expressed in simple yet profound phrases like "I just want you to be the type of child I can be proud of," was a powerful motivator for me to strive to be just that.

My mother, who was deeply involved in the family funeral business, often worked long hours and always had to respond to calls. Despite her demanding schedule, she was unwavering in ensuring that we were well-fed with nutritious meals and that our routines remained consistent. She was a virtuoso in balancing her professional responsibilities with family life, adeptly meeting all our basic needs. From her, I learned invaluable lessons in communication and the importance of articulating my needs and preferences. She showed immense trust in me, allowing me to drive the family Cadillac as soon as I could legally, a testament to her confidence in my sense of responsibility.

During my teenage years, my mother's approach shifted to a more stringent style, likely driven by her desire to steer me on the right path. She imposed what I then perceived as unreasonable curfews and restrictions, such as not allowing boys in the house when adults were absent and avoiding certain areas with unsavory reputations. However, her rules were fundamentally aimed at instilling respect and responsibility in me, striving to keep me safe.

Her humility shone through in her interactions, often understating my accomplishments in conversations with friends. Her exposure to grief and loss in her profession fostered exceptional compassion and empathy, qualities she generously extended to my brother and me.

As I grew older, I sensed a change in our relationship. My mother's protective instincts sometimes seemed at odds with my burgeoning independence. While I understood her concerns, I sometimes felt confined by her traditional views on what it meant to be a "lady," which occasionally seemed to hinder my pursuit of enjoyment. Nevertheless, we shared common aspirations: academic excellence, the pursuit of higher education, and the value of independence. Our relationship evolved and matured once I embarked on my college journey, as she witnessed me confidently navigate the path that we both cherished.

This introspection on my upbringing underscores the intricate and dynamic fabric of parenting. It reflects the influence of generational experiences, personal beliefs, and the evolving societal landscape. The blend of guidance, trust, and structure that my parents provided has been a foundational element that I have carried into my approach to parenting and now observe with a keen interest in the upbringing of my grandchildren.

My Style

My fascination with human behavior and the intricate workings of the mind began at a very young age, sparking a deep curiosity that eventually led me to major in psychology. This academic pursuit was the first step in a journey that would later see me embarking on a career as a psychiatric social worker. This professional path enhanced my understanding of the complexities of human emotions and actions and solidified my interest in observing and interpreting the nuances of people's behaviors, overt and covert communications, and the diverse experiences that shaped their lives for the better or worse.

Looking back at my parents' parenting style, it's unclear whether they had a meticulously planned approach to raising children. Yet, as early as the age of thirteen, I often pondered over what kind of parent I wanted to be. I had grasped the significance of living a disciplined life, the value of formal education, and the necessity of having a stable career to support myself and, eventually, my future family.

As I experienced my first pregnancy, I was deeply immersed in thoughts about parenting. My academic background exposed me to various psychological theories and the insights of renowned behaviorists. I was determined to blend the best elements of my parents' approach with my improvements and insights. I greatly appreciated how they kept me engaged in social activities, and I sought to provide my children with even more enriching and diverse experiences.

As someone trained in the art of listening, I was particularly attentive to what my children said and what they left unsaid. I often looked into their eyes, trying to understand their unspoken thoughts and feelings. This approach was somewhat different from my parents, who tended to wait for me to initiate conversations about my emotions. In contrast, I proactively inquired about my children's interests, dislikes, and desires, always listening attentively and endeavoring to fulfill their reasonable requests.

Like my parents, I prided myself on being a hard worker, but I also consciously made time to be active in my children's lives. I was always there to support my daughters, celebrating their achievements more expressively than I had experienced in my childhood. For example, I rewarded Danielle with communication devices for her excellent report cards. I acknowledged Candice's generosity, such as sharing her orchestra earnings, by matching her contribution and giving it back to her.

In guiding my children, I often chose a more indirect approach, especially regarding behaviors I preferred they avoid. While my mother was more direct in her instructions during my teenage years, I created an environment that naturally discouraged certain behaviors. For instance, I allowed my children to use the phone as they wished, understanding it was a regular part of teenage life, provided they were safe at home. This was a marked contrast to the strict phone use rules I had as a teenager.

Regarding household responsibilities like keeping their rooms clean, I initially set the exact expectations I had grown up with. However, when Danielle expressed her reluctance to adhere strictly to this rule, I respected her honesty and autonomy, a significant departure from the approach I would have taken with my parents.

Reflecting on my journey as a parent, it's evident that my style was a carefully considered amalgam, aiming to avoid some of my parents' less beneficial practices while embracing and enhancing their positive aspects. This introspection highlights the evolution of my parenting style, influenced by a combination of personal experiences, professional knowledge, and a desire to create a nurturing, understanding, and supportive environment for my children.

My Daughter's Style

Candice, a dedicated mother to two remarkable children—(as of this date) an eleven-year-old daughter and an eight-year-old son—seeks my counsel on various topics. These range from career decisions and parenting strategies to friendships and everyday challenges. It's incredibly heartwarming and fills me with immense pride that she holds my opinions in such high esteem. This is a notable contrast to her teenage years, typical of most teenagers, where she might not have valued my views as profoundly.

Candice frequently shares anecdotes about her children, and in these stories, she reflects on how she often finds herself guided by the advice and lessons I imparted, especially when she faces parenting hurdles. She actively engages her children in sports and social activities, mirroring how I involved her in her youth. Going a step beyond, she regularly asks about her children's preferences in these activities, demonstrating an initiative and attentiveness that I deeply respect and echo how she was brought up. When it comes to rewarding her children, she exhibits a level of generosity that surpasses my practices. For example, in recognition of their progress in swimming—a skill I ensured she and her sister acquired from a young age. Candice surprised her children with an exciting trip to Hawaii!

She benefits from the flexibility of working from home, which allows her to monitor her children's internet usage closely. This vigilant oversight helps to shield them from potential online dangers, a precaution that wasn't as accessible to me when they were growing up. I remember being particularly careful about monitoring Danielle's internet use during her teenage years, always supervising her online activities and educating her about responsible internet usage.

Candice similarly engages in talks with her children about the internet and social media, teaching them to navigate these complex realms wisely. She is raising her children with foundational values and strengths similar to those I tried to instill in her, equipping them with robust self-esteem and resilience to face life's challenges. The significant time and effort invested in their early years have fortified them against the vulnerabilities and pitfalls of social media.

Whenever my grandchildren visit, I dedicate my time to imparting the same life lessons I shared with Candice and Danielle. It's a rewarding experience to pass down these teachings to another generation, and Candice greatly values my involvement in her children's development.

Although she doesn't have children, Danielle often shares with me how the values and principles I taught resonate in her daily life. The virtues of kindness, respect, patience, and understanding, which she attributes to my influence, are evident in her interactions with others. This transference of values from generation to generation fills me with a profound sense of fulfillment and joy.

Reflecting on the evolution of parenting across these three generations, each era has contributed its own valuable lessons. My parents instilled the importance of structure, discipline, and quiet yet profound expressions of love. My own parenting journey emphasized the necessity of open communication, adaptability, and fostering critical thinking. Observing Candice, I am learning about the intricacies of emotional intelligence and the unique challenges of parenting in a digital era.

Each generation adds its distinct perspective, shaped by the unique challenges and resources available during its time. However, at the heart of it all lies a deep, unwavering love for our children and a unified aspiration to see them grow into happy, fulfilled, and compassionate individuals, thriving in their respective journeys.

Candice, me, and Danielle at my wedding

11

Performing a Self-Evaluation

Embarking on the parenting journey, it's essential to occasionally take a step back and critically assess the PPP and your adherence to it. This self-evaluation is crucial, as it illuminates areas where the plan may not be producing the anticipated outcomes. This process isn't about fixating on the negatives but acknowledging and embracing the fluidity and adaptability of a well-structured parenting plan. It's designed to be a living, evolving guide that grows and changes not only with your children but also with shifts in your personal and professional life.

I fondly recall a memorable evening spent with one of my dearest elementary school friends, joined by my two daughters, at a local restaurant. The night was filled with laughter and engaging conversations. During the meal, I indulged in a Margarita, my preferred beverage, and found myself quite relaxed and joyous. My children, who were more accustomed to seeing me in a serious and task-focused manner, often operating in "survival mode" and juggling multiple responsibilities, were taken aback. They misinterpreted my joviality for intoxication, as they had rarely seen this more light-hearted and carefree side of me. That insight came to light later when they shared that they often sought emotional support elsewhere, as they had seldom experienced this more relaxed aspect of my personality.

Navigating through the teenage years of parenting brings its own set of unique challenges. I remember a particularly intense argument with Candice, a standout sprinter on her high school track team. Although the specifics of the disagreement have faded over time, the intensity of that moment remains clear. The situation escalated to the point where, in a rare moment of loss of composure, I ended up chasing after her. Fortuitously, her athletic skills meant she could easily outrun me, which thankfully gave me a moment to cool down and collect my thoughts.

In the heat of that pursuit, I reminded myself of my deep love for her, reinforcing the thought that causing her any distress was the furthest thing from my intentions. This incident was a powerful lesson in the importance of maintaining calm and control, especially in escalating situations, to avoid inadvertently harming your children or straining the parent-child relationship.

These personal experiences highlight the significance of creating a parenting plan and living it in a manner attuned to the needs and welfare of both the parent and the child. It's about finding a harmonious balance between enforcing discipline and allowing for moments of joy, relaxation, and vulnerability. Remember, regularly revisiting and tweaking the PPP in response to new experiences and insights is vital to ensure that it continues to serve as a relevant and practical compass in your dynamic and ever-evolving parenting journey.

Some Basic Truths

Navigating through life, we encounter elements beyond our control, and embracing this truth is a fundamental part of our journey. It's a fact that the circumstances of our birth—the time, the place, and the environment—were not of our choosing. Similarly, we don't have the dominion to command natural elements like the sun or the rain. While it's often stated that death and taxes are the inescapable constants of life, the attitude we adopt toward these inevitabilities can profoundly influence our experience.

Consider the weather as an example. On sunny days, we can shield ourselves with hats and sunscreen, turning a potentially harmful situation into a manageable one. In times of excessive heat, we can find solace in air-conditioned environments, adapting our surroundings to suit our comfort. Rain, too, can be navigated with an umbrella, keeping us dry and untroubled. In a similar vein, while death is an unavoidable part of life, the choices we make can significantly impact the timing and quality of our lives. Leading a healthy lifestyle, for instance, may fend off illness and extend our lifespan.

A proactive approach to taxes can be equally beneficial. Keeping abreast of changing tax laws, consulting with a Certified Public Accountant (CPA), and managing finances astutely can ease the burden they present, turning a seemingly unavoidable stressor into a manageable part of life.

The same principles of control and surrender apply when raising a family. This can be likened to a game of cards. In this game, we're dealt various cards – some are inherently advantageous, while others require strategic play to yield success. There may be cards that initially appear less favorable, but with thoughtful planning and execution, they, too, can contribute to a triumphant outcome.

The essence lies in doing our best; perfection is an elusive goal. It's important to minimize regret and guilt, as dwelling on these can be energetically draining and distracting from other enriching aspects of life.

Reflecting on my journey, particularly in my background in human behavior and my role as a hospital administrator, I realize there were times when I perhaps overly controlled my emotions. This learned behavior stemmed from my professional environment, where impulsive, emotionally driven decisions were often discouraged in favor of objectivity and rationality. This approach also permeated my parenting style, where I frequently emphasized pragmatic and rational decision-making. This reflection offers insight into the delicate balance between control, acceptance, and the ongoing learning process inherent in parenting and life.

Memorable Moments

My journey as a parent has been adorned with countless moments of pride and joy, witnessing the growth and achievements of my children. From the moment of their births, I was steadfast in my commitment to providing them with every possible opportunity to ensure their successful graduation from college. I often visualized them adorned in graduation caps and gowns, symbols of the accomplishments and success that my guidance and their hard work were directed toward achieving.

A particularly proud milestone was when Candice was accepted into the University of Michigan. This institution holds a special place in our family as the alma mater of my first and second husbands and myself. The University of Michigan's reputation as an excellent school intensified my joy upon her admission. Despite the daunting cost of college tuition, estimated at around $120,000 for a four-year course, Candice, demonstrating her independence and initiative, applied and received early acceptance during her senior year of high school. She was notably offered a partial scholarship which was well-received and put to good use. She was recognized as the fastest sprinter in her high school.

When I was attending the new student orientation with her, there was a speaker who highlighted the rigors and challenges of academic life, mentioning that not all students graduate within four years. In response, I gently reminded Candice, seated beside me, of my commitment to support her through only four years of college. True to her dedication and capabilities, she graduated within this timeframe.

Reflecting on these moments allows me to appreciate the immense joys and pride that come with parenting. For example, Danielle displayed her academic excellence by getting all A's on her report card following a semester of focused discussions and hard work.

A vivid memory from Candice's middle school years involved a parent-teacher meeting where she confidently challenged her grade. She presented well-calculated averages to the teacher, illustrating that she deserved a higher mark. Upon verification, the teacher acknowledged the accuracy of her calculations and amended the grade. This experience reinforced the value of accountability and self-advocacy for both of us.

Music, a personal passion, was also a field that my daughters enjoyed. Listening to them practice and perform in duets with their piano teacher or solo recitals always filled me with immense happiness and pride. In fact, Candice's accomplishments extended well beyond the academic realm. She performed a violin solo with the Atlanta Symphony Orchestra and participated in a Friendship Tour to China. Their musical journey instilled in them the values of dedication and practice, and they knew how proud I was of their talents.

Embodying natural leadership qualities, Danielle was popular among her peers and represented her cheerleading squad in the Ms. Raiders contest in high school. Her vocal talents shone as she performed solos, including singing the National Anthem at a basketball game. Her passion for dance, which she had nurtured since age two, led her to join a competitive dance group, winning numerous competitions. At the University of Florida, she was crowned Homecoming Queen and continued our family legacy by pledging Alpha Kappa Alpha. She later completed her master's degree at the University of Texas, which paved the way for her current role as a Sr. Vice President.

These experiences, replete with joy and a deep sense of accomplishment, stand as a testament to the rewarding nature of parenting. They exemplify the fulfillment that comes from seeing your children succeed, thrive, and carve their unique paths in life.

A Parent With Purpose

Embracing the role of a single parent to two daughters while navigating a demanding career was a transformative experience that reshaped me into a better person. This journey imbued me with invaluable skills such as time management, effective communication with both children and adults, event organization, and, most crucially, patience. My dedicated adherence to my parenting plan was instrumental in reaping these personal benefits.

One vivid example is the annual organization of Danielle's birthday sleepovers, which demanded meticulous planning and execution. Tasks ranged from sending out invitations and preparing the house to organizing refreshments while balancing my professional responsibilities. These experiences refined my skills in event planning and organization, attributes that have continued to serve me well in various aspects of my life.

For me, perhaps the most transformative lesson from this journey was learning patience. Before becoming a mother, I was not especially known for this virtue. I used to rush through tasks, eager to complete them swiftly. However, the act of parenting fundamentally alters one's approach to life. For nine years, I consistently reminded Danielle about the importance of saying "please" and "thank you," firmly sticking to my plan. This perseverance bore fruit as she grew to be exceptionally polite, demonstrating the value of persistence and inner strength. The success and happiness of my daughters have been immense sources of joy for me, highlighting the profoundly positive impact that parenting has had on my life.

Witnessing my children's accomplishments as adults is one of my life's greatest joys. For instance, visiting Candice at her law firm and seeing her in action as a practicing attorney fills me with immense pride. Similarly, observing Danielle's adept teaching skills during a visit to her classroom left me equally impressed and proud.

From their early years, I have always encouraged them to embrace their individuality, assuring them of their intelligence and capabilities. They grew up in an environment that equipped them to approach challenges with a belief in finding solutions. They learned to analyze situations, navigate difficulties, and maintain a well-balanced life.

Another dimension of evaluating the well-being of adult children is through the conversations we share. I am aware that life is transient, so I have endeavored to desensitize them to my aging process. Humor has played a pivotal role in our interactions. For instance, there was a light-hearted moment when Danielle playfully suggested that I had lost my mind a long time ago, leading to a session of shared laughter and warmth.

Candice recently relayed a compliment from a cousin who admired the positive behavioral model I had set over the years and expressed a desire to emulate it with her children. This acknowledgment was significant and affirming to me.

As my children transitioned into adulthood, their independence and sense of humor brought me considerable relief and joy. A memorable incident involved Danielle humorously threatening to remove me from our shared Verizon account due to high costs, a situation that ended in laughter and her graciously allowing me to remain on the plan.

Me enjoying an early evening out

12

Managing the Hand We're Dealt

In my journey as a parent, there were countless early Saturday mornings when I would rise before the first light of dawn. These mornings were dedicated to tidying up the house, creating a welcoming and orderly environment before my daughters awoke for their track meets. These moments I often followed weeks brimming with professional challenges and exhaustion. In the quiet of those mornings, the radio would play softly in the background, its melodies often fading into the background of my preoccupied mind.

Yet, one such morning, the song "Rescue Me" began to play. Its melodious tune and heartfelt lyrics seemed to speak directly to me, infusing me with a newfound strength and resolve to face the day ahead. I was conscientious about shielding my children from these burdens during stress or pressure. They seldom saw me overtaken by emotion or impulsivity; I was steadfast in navigating any challenging situation, ensuring my stress never impacted them.

Reflecting, I recall how my father introduced me to the inspiring *Song of Bernadette* during my childhood. Whenever life's challenges seemed overwhelming, I would think of Bernadette's journey. Her story of enduring severe trials as a peasant girl with a profound vision put my struggles into perspective, reminding me that my hardships were comparatively less severe.

As I've mentioned periodically, I like metaphors, particularly equating life's challenges to playing cards. I categorized these cards as winners, losers, and middle cards. The winning cards in my life were treasured—a nurturing family, a solid education, robust health, a love for learning, supportive friends, healthy children, and my basic needs always being met. These assets provided me with resilience and were sometimes the result of fortunate circumstances, such as being born into a loving family.

In facing the inevitable "losing cards" in life, my strategy was to recognize these challenges and devise plans to move forward and mitigate their adverse effects. The "middle cards" were the ones with potential—akin to a hand in a game of poker or bidding, where they could be transformed into winners with strategic play and the right approach. This euphemism of a deck of cards allowed me to visualize and better comprehend various life scenarios. This categorization, prioritization, and minimization method effectively helped me manage life's varied challenges.

Creating a personal set of mental images or compiling a list of favorite movies, books, or songs can be a grounding technique for you as well. These resources have helped me regain focus and perspective during challenging times, just as they might offer solace and clarity to others.

When nurturing honesty in my children, I've always emphasized the importance of truthfulness. I assured them that honesty would lead to better outcomes, even when the truth might be hard to share. Lies and secrets, I believed, were counterproductive. As a parent, I learned the importance of not reacting immediately to unpleasant news, giving my children the space and grace to share their truths, thereby encouraging open dialogue. They did not need to fear my reaction. Addressing issues appropriately while always considering their best interests was a practice that required some effort but was unquestionably worthwhile. I wanted my children to understand that honesty wouldn't lead to punishment—a fear that often keeps children from being open with their parents. Ensuring a comfortable environment for sharing is vital, as it allows parents to help with their children's challenges effectively.

Adhering to my parenting plan became a daily habit. The meticulously crafted plan served as a guide and reminder for me to stay on track with my parenting goals. Recognizing that to prioritize my children, I needed to be my best self—healthy, happy, and strong—was integral to the success of my plan. That took on renewed importance following my divorce and my transition to being a single parent. Updating and adapting my plan in light of this significant life change was necessary and empowering. Continuing with my life without a partner, I knew the journey would be demanding. Yet, I remained confident that the solutions and strength needed would emerge over time as long as I stayed committed and focused.

My reflections on the experience of parenting, including everything from the delight of early mornings with young children to the careful planning needed to navigate life's various obstacles, underscore the fulfilling path of raising a family. This journey not only brings joy but also fosters significant personal development. My lifelong goal has always been to live a life of purpose, to be remembered as a person of integrity who helped others, and above all, to make my children feel proud of me.

It's a familiar scenario where teenagers might feel a sense of embarrassment about their parents, but as they grow into adulthood, they often come to realize and value the love and effort that went into their upbringing. The approach I took in parenting aimed to imbue them with the confidence to face life's challenges head-on, to express their opinions boldly, and to be successful in whatever they pursue. For me, the adventure of parenting, replete with its love, difficulties, and victories, remains a continual source of deep satisfaction and fulfillment.

My Champion Airedale, Bryce, was with me as I wrote this book

13

Lessons Learned

Watching celebrities on TV share their personal stories, I'm struck by the recurring themes of overcoming significant challenges — obesity, drug addiction, and depression, to name a few. These narratives are undeniably inspiring, portraying resilience and hope. This observation led me to ponder: What if we could not only share life lessons for overcoming adversities but also provide guidance to avoid these hardships in the first place? What if these stories could act as a roadmap for a life that's not just free from unnecessary struggles but also enriched with purpose and fulfillment? This concept is at the heart of what I aim to impart in this book.

Embarking on a purposeful life is a transformative journey that deeply influences both ourselves and those around us. It begins with a critical and life-altering concept: self-awareness. Knowing oneself—your values, dreams, and distinct purpose—lays the groundwork for this journey. In a world inundated with external pressures, it's all too easy to lose sight of our true selves. We might find ourselves merely reacting to life's events rather than actively shaping our destiny. However, I am convinced that self-awareness empowers us to avoid drifting aimlessly and instead live with deliberate intention and direction.

Another essential step on this path is establishing clear goals and objectives. Like a ship adrift without a destination, a life without goals is directionless. By setting well-defined goals, we chart our course, taking control and navigating toward our desired future with purpose and determination.

For those reflecting on their past, remember it's never too late to influence your future. Examining your past, especially your formative years and family dynamics, can provide priceless insights. It allows you to recognize the forces that have shaped you and to consciously decide which aspects of your upbringing to embrace or alter. This process is an opportunity to rebuild your life's foundation, deciding what to keep and what to evolve.

While some may choose to emulate their parents' life paths, it's important to realize the power you hold to carve out your own unique journey, one that aligns with your vision of a fulfilling life. This often involves breaking away from outdated patterns and forging a distinct legacy.

This evolution I'm describing extends beyond mere self-improvement; it encompasses a broader spectrum of enhancing how we connect and engage with those around us. When we cultivate self-awareness, we unlock the ability to communicate more effectively. This enhanced communication is not just about conveying our thoughts more clearly; it's about truly understanding and empathizing with others. With self-awareness, we also develop resilience to face life's challenges. This resilience allows us to meet obstacles not with fear or avoidance but with a strength informed by our deepest values and beliefs. Also, self-awareness guides us in making decisions that are not just reactive or spontaneous but are deeply rooted in our core values.

Reflecting on my experiences as a parent, I've observed a fascinating evolution in parenting styles across different generations. This introspection has been enlightening, helping me better comprehend the choices I made as a parent and how these choices have influenced the way my children now navigate their own lives. I share these reflections with the hope that they will inspire you to embark on a similar journey of self-discovery and introspective analysis. This process involves setting personal goals, making conscious choices, and understanding oneself on a deeper level. By undertaking this journey, you might discover your own route to a life that is purposefully designed to be both meaningful and fulfilling.

Regardless of where you are in your journey—whether you're a parent managing the complexities of family life, a single professional navigating your career, or someone transitioning through different life stages—the path toward a life of purpose is always accessible. It's a journey marked by self-discovery, where you learn about your true desires, aspirations, and motivations. It's about intentionality, where actions and decisions are made with a clear purpose and goal in mind. It's a journey of transformation, where you gradually evolve into a person who lives each day with a sense of purpose, making choices and engaging in interactions that are all steps toward a meaningful existence.

As you embark on this journey, you'll find that the most satisfying and rewarding life is one that is lived intentionally. It's a life where each day is approached not as a random series of events but as a deliberate journey toward achieving something greater. Every choice you make, every interaction you have, becomes part of a larger narrative of a life lived with purpose and intention. This journey of purposeful living doesn't just bring personal satisfaction; it also has the power to positively impact those around you, creating a ripple effect of positivity and purpose.

Danielle and Candice visiting my home in Detroit

14

Was It Worth It?

Throughout my parenting journey, a significant moment caused me to pause and deeply reflect on my experiences and the choices I had made. It's a question that perhaps all parents consider at some point: if given the opportunity, would I choose to embark on this parenting journey again? For about twenty-one years, until my younger daughter turned eighteen, my life took a path that was far more enriching and complex than I could have ever anticipated, primarily shaped by the joys and challenges of raising my two daughters.

A particularly heartwarming chapter in this journey unfolded when my adult daughters orchestrated a surprise birthday celebration for me at a luxurious private club. The event, planned secretly and held after my actual birthday, caught me completely off guard. They had cleverly collaborated with my husband, who convinced me to go to the venue under the pretense of meeting a friend. My hesitation quickly turned to astonishment and sheer joy as I entered the room, greeted by exuberant shouts of "Surprise!" from friends, family, and my cherished grandchildren. I was led to a place of honor near the head of the table, where I was surrounded by loved ones who took turns sharing heartfelt stories and anecdotes about moments in my life that had significantly impacted them.

Listening to these stories, some of which I had long forgotten, was an extraordinary and humbling experience. It's remarkable to realize how certain actions and gestures, which may have seemed minor at the time, can leave such profound and lasting impressions on the lives of others. The stories varied from humorous recollections of my efforts to maintain decorum during my children's prom nights to more touching memories of my long drives to support friends in need. My daughters fondly recalled visiting me at work and witnessing how I interacted with everyone with dignity and respect. The term "kind" was a recurring theme in their narratives, underscoring the enduring impact of kindness. This surprise birthday party was not merely a celebration of my age but a touching homage to the life I had led and the values I had imparted.

In the realm of parenting, finding the right balance between trust and structure is essential. Providing a stable environment with established routines offers children a sense of security and predictability, which is crucial for their development. I always tried to discuss decisions that directly affected my children, ensuring they felt included and valued in the family dynamics. This approach was exemplified by our open conversations, like when Candice expressed feelings of boredom, highlighting the importance of our routine of open dialogue.

Allowing children to make their own decisions and learn from their mistakes is an indispensable part of their growth. It equips them with crucial decision-making skills and the ability to learn from experiences, thus reducing the likelihood of repeating mistakes as they mature.

Exposing children to a diverse range of experiences is also critical. Activities such as attending concerts, participating in sports events, visiting parks, and traveling can significantly broaden their horizons. Such exposure is vital for children to discover their passions and interests. Observing their reactions to various activities can also be a window into their potential talents and inclinations.

When my daughters, grandchildren, and I planned a trip to Marietta, GA, where they spent their formative years, the entire process reflected our family's approach to life. As the initiator, I began researching and planning months in advance, involving my daughters in the planning through Zoom meetings. We meticulously organized every aspect of our trip, from synchronizing our arrival times to choosing suitable clothing and accommodations. This resulted in an eight-page detailed itinerary, demonstrating how thorough planning has been a fundamental aspect of our lives, enabling us to maximize our experiences.

During the trip, as I sat between my grandchildren in the SUV, I listened intently to my daughters as they exchanged professional and personal insights. Their conversation, rich with wisdom, filled me with immense pride. They spoke of how the upbringing I provided had positively influenced them, expressing appreciation for their strong sisterly bond and the solid foundation they received.

Reflecting on their childhood activities, from participating in sports to being involved in various clubs, I realized how those early experiences had stayed with them. Candice, for example, ensures her children are involved in sports and music, drawing from her own childhood experiences. Danielle maintains a regular exercise routine, a habit instilled from an early age. My daughters' continued healthy and active lifestyles are a testament to their upbringing.

Recently, when I was talking to Candice on the phone, I overheard her interacting with her children after picking them up from a summer chess camp. Their lively discussion about the day's events, including navigating a challenging situation with another child, was a heartwarming moment. Her approach mirrored my own, illustrating how my parenting style had been embraced and adapted by her in raising her children.

This moment was a profound affirmation of my parenting journey. It was a clear demonstration of how the values, lessons, and styles I had imparted were now influencing not just my children but also my grandchildren. This journey, replete with its various challenges and victories, has been an enriching and fulfilling experience. It continues to bring me joy and pride as I witness the lasting impact of my parenting across generations!

Was It Easy?

It is essential to realize that your life will not be the same if you are serious about having the type of children you desire. It will probably be necessary to make sacrifices and alter your lifestyle to devote time and resources to raising a family.

The simple answer is "NO." This was the most challenging, most difficult part of my life! There were so many nights that I could not sleep trying to figure out what I needed to do to balance my job and the needs of the children. During the day or when I was driving, I was working through difficult situations and how best to resolve them. Being consistent every year after year was a daunting task. The stress and anxiety were constant. I tried never to show my struggle to my two girls. I was so concerned about doing my best that it almost consumed me. It took all my energy and everything within me to stay the course. Knowing myself and how committed I tend to be once I decide, especially as important as raising these two girls as a single parent, and knowing how at risk I was, according to the statistics, was a significant part of my thinking. I knew that this was going to be my life. I can remember praying to God, asking that I live long enough and have the strength to raise my girls even though it was so difficult for me. Looking back, I did not ask God to make my life easier. I firmly believed that what I was doing was the best. I did not think it could be more accessible. I was focused on the outcome no matter what the cost was to me.

I can remember I would go to the bank that was close to one of the hospitals where I was working. I would complete the withdrawal slip, take it to the cashier, and leave before she had the time to give me the money! I was in such a hurry that this happened to me several times. I was always playing "Beat the Clock." Once I realized I had left the bank before I got the money, I would return to the bank where they held it for me. That is how often that occurred.

It was not until my daughters were adults that I realized that the pressure I was under all those years did have some unintended impact on them. As I thought about it, they had probably never seen me laugh; they had never seen me happy and relaxed. I realized I had been so focused on doing things in their best interest that I could never relax and be satisfied. Immediately, I changed my countenance, and from that moment on, I laughed and showed I was happy.

As a single mom for most of my children's lives, I felt like I was sacrificing everything I used to enjoy. It seemed like time was moving so slowly. I tried not to think about all the activities I gave up to save time and money. I gave up my favorite sports, tennis and horseback riding, which I truly missed. I had always liked dogs and could not have a dog because I did not have time to care for one. A dog must be fed, walked, played with, trained, taken to the doctor, etc. I could barely care for my two girls and work a demanding job. I would not marry again because I knew that there was a huge probability that there would be problems with the children adjusting to a new father. I had very definite viewpoints and values of how best to raise children. I had a parenting plan! Chances would be that a new husband would not abide by my wishes. Adjusting to any new person in the family would be monumental for me. I was already too tired. Financial responsibilities forced me to be frugal. Ebenezer Scrooge had nothing on me!

I taught myself to economize to the extreme. I did not have to wear make-up. I could do my hair most of the time. I did not have to shop at Nordstrom or Saks Fifth Avenue. Marshall's, T.J. Maxx, consignment stores, and Stein Mart were the stores I frequented when I needed something to wear. Even though I have always been health conscious, it did not motivate me to stay at my normal size and weight. There was no way I would gain weight because I would have to buy more clothes.

What is interesting as I look back over the years, now that my children are adults and making more money than I ever did, my frugal habits have stayed the same. Time seems to have gone so fast now that my child-rearing responsibilities are over. I am still reusing items, staying at the same clothes and weight size, and not desiring anything that I consider over-priced. The Dollar Store is still my favorite store. My walking buddy and I had our usual daily walk in the park. She listened to me, telling me the type of life I was living. I was satisfied with my frugal life. She observed that I had gone to the extreme more than when the children were young. That was her observation. She said, "Carol, you don't have to live like a pauper!"

I was finally able to get married once the children were adults. I could adjust because I was retired, and the children were adults living out of state with good jobs. Getting remarried requires time, effort, and compromise. I finally had the time! I was not so overwhelmed with raising my two girls, so I had the energy! My new husband was wonderful, and I was glad I waited because I was able to be a devoted wife. He already had two adult children, and our families were able to merge and get along.

Getting a dog was one of my previous sacrifices. I always wanted to have a dog, but now I could. There was no way I could adequately take care of a dog when the children were growing up. I did not have the time or the energy. I never wanted to mistreat or neglect a dog. My husband, Chris, and I got a handsome male Airedale Terrier. We named him Bryce. He is an excellent companion and keeps me company, especially when my husband is out of town. He is also a good deterrent for preventing crime. He has the loudest bark when anyone comes near the house.

In the first training class I took him to, one of the people who showed dogs in competitions said he was a winner! True to form, I entered Bryce in show competitions. It was challenging and took a lot of work, but that was right down my alley. He became a champion as a show dog and a therapy dog. We would go to a children's hospital and bring cheer to the children and the staff.

Since I did not have any boys, he was my boy, and I will admit I did not follow a "parenting plan." I was able to treat him differently. As my husband says, I spoiled the dog. He thinks Bryce gets more attention than he does.

I admit I do things for him that I never did for my girls. This is the reason. A dog will always be dependent on its owner. He doesn't have to pass tests to go to college, he won't have to get a paying job, he won't have to buy a house, raise children, go shopping for groceries, etc. I can use baby talk on him, which I would never do with my girls. Bryce taught me how to spend money, too. When it comes to what Bryce needs, there are no limits! Of course, my husband and girls always point that out to me. My husband has said that if he is reincarnated, he wants to return as my dog! I was able to be my authentic self with Bryce.

Traveling was another sacrifice I made. Any traveling I did was for the benefit of the children if it was not job-related. We could take short trips usually associated with their sports or concerts. Traveling was limited while working because I could not get enough time off. International travel for my daughters, which their schools did not provide, was just not feasible for me. Fortunately, my girls could travel internationally because their schools had study-abroad programs.

Going to Machu Picchu was a place I had always wanted to visit. It was an old civilization in South Peru that the Spanish conquistadores did not even know existed because it was so well hidden. When the children were growing up, it would have been unthinkable for me to travel that far and take my daughters. After the girls were adults, my new husband said he would accompany me. I wanted to stay at the Sanctuary Lodge at the foot of the mountains near the entrance to this historic city. I was outraged when I found out it would cost over $1000 per night. I was complaining to my children about how expensive it was. I was ranting and raving and did not want to pay all that money. Both of my girls had a good long talk with me. They explained I had not spent any money on what I wanted for years. I deserved to enjoy myself because I had looked forward to taking this trip. After many conversations, I did reserve the hotel...but for only one night!

I remember parents from my girls' high school giving me words of wisdom at their fifth and last daughter's high school graduation. These parents were so calm and seemed so wise. I knew they had been confronted with every possible situation with their family. The father said life is like a highway. Before children come along, the thoroughfare is paved and relatively smooth going. Once they are born, you have taken a detour, and that detour is unpaved, with many potholes and rough terrain. After the children leave home, you can return to the paved highway and continue your life. However, you are still a parent and will never be as carefree as before the children were born.

Life does get easier once they leave home and you have raised them to the best of your ability. The detour in the road was another good metaphor for my life. That detour was rough and challenging, but we all survived! I learned so much from this detour. It is good to be back on the paved road again!

Ayanna, Danielle, me, Candice, and Chris in Hawaii celebrating our 10th wedding anniversary

Epilogue

Writing this book has been an immensely fulfilling experience, largely due to the rewarding Zoom conversations with my adult daughters. The standout feature of these dialogues was their perceptive analysis and critique of the parenting techniques I used during their upbringing. A notable insight from these discussions was their observation that few of their friends' parents engaged in such reflective conversations. They realized that their upbringing was quite unique compared to their peers. These conversations also brought to light the differences in our memories of certain events, uncovering instances where our recollections diverged, particularly in moments of selective memory about various incidents. Despite some constructive criticism, both daughters concurred that the parenting methods I employed had a positive impact on their lives, equipping them to tackle life's challenges confidently.

I have always considered parenting the most critical role in my life, a sentiment that carries no negative connotation. Rather, it underscores that parenting, like any professional endeavor, demands preparation, training, patience, thoughtfulness, and time. Similar to the expectations in a professional role, parenting comes with its own unique responsibilities and expectations. My background in human behavior and psychology significantly enriched the quality of my parenting and aided in the development of a plan designed to optimize my children's chances of success.

I often reflect on how my parenting approach might have differed if I were a single parent of a boy or raised children in a two-parent home. I believe that my fundamental approach would have remained consistent. I would have striven to understand the unique needs of a boy, drawing on insights from other parents and my own experiences growing up with a father and brother. Additionally, managing a relationship with a husband would introduce another dynamic to consider. Despite their different personalities, my daughters were largely subject to the same rules, with individual accommodations made as necessary.

Since my daughters were so active in extracurricular activities, I wondered how that might impact their adult lives. It would have been devastating if they had said they felt it was a waste of time, and fortunately, that did not happen. However, it's natural to wonder if putting in all of that time, effort, and money pays off in the end. When we embark on those journeys, we never know what the outcome will be.

Fortunately for me, it's incredibly rewarding to see my grandchildren now engaged in similar activities. They have taken an interest in sports and music, likely inspired by their mother's childhood involvement. I hope Candice's ability to help and support them in these areas is a testament to what I did for her. For instance, Grayson, at eight years old, not only plays the piano but also composes his own music, enjoys basketball, soccer, baseball, and tennis, and shows promise as an athlete. Jordyn is passionate about soccer, reading, and dancing and has recently started learning the violin. Observing their joy and growth in these activities is truly gratifying.

Ultimately, the essence of parenting lies in doing the best one can and acknowledging one's strengths and weaknesses as part of the human journey. My relationship with my daughters has evolved to a point where our communication is effortless and authentic. They understand my intentions clearly, fostering a relationship free from the constraints of cautiousness around egos. We now enjoy friendly competitions and share countless joyful moments together, further enriching our bond.

This sentiment was encapsulated in a text from Danielle on September 5, 2022, which read: "Mummy! Just thinking about you. I love you so much and am so lucky you raised me. Thank you for being an incredible human and an even more amazing mom!"

That message affirmed my belief: indeed, every effort, every challenge, and every moment spent parenting was undoubtedly worth it.

Acknowledgements

I am forever thankful to the many people who enabled me to write this book. First, I want to thank my two daughters, Candice and Danielle, who were so hilarious on our Zoom sessions (one lives in Texas, and the other lives in California) as we tested our memories of how they were raised. I must also give recognition to my Airedale Terrier, Bryce, who sat with me early in the mornings when I wrote chapters of my book. Bryce sat quietly at my feet, waiting for me to take him for a walk.

There were many people who encouraged me to write a book about how I parented my two girls. Some were family, colleagues, friends and many I talked with over the phone. Some parents that I never really met in person remembered years later that they had followed the advice I gave them over the phone. It was their excitement about this book that motivated me to keep writing. My grandchildren were instrumental in letting me know that my techniques for raising children are intergenerational. I could see that my daughters were raising their children as I raised them. My third daughter, Ayanna, (my second husband's daughter) who has two children, could appreciate the benefits of my method of raising children even though it was different.

Many thanks to my agent, Diane Nine. She has years of experience and saw value in the message I wanted to share in this book. A special thanks goes to David Smitherman for his advice and counsel as I created this book.

Rand-Smith, my publisher, is responsible for having the vision to think this book was worth publishing.

I always felt I had a story to tell, and I tried to write this book in a literary way.

A heartfelt gratitude go to my dearest friends who helped with the initial stages of compiling the chapters in my book. Margo Williams, Linda King, and Rita Riddle were there for me, reading through the rough drafts and always encouraging me. They continue to offer any support that I need.

Finally, this has been an exciting journey. It is a new path full of opportunities to learn.

About the Author

Born and raised in St. Louis, MO, I hail from a family where education and professionalism were paramount. My father, a high school teacher, and my mother, an adept funeral director managing our family-owned business, both held college degrees when it was less common than today, especially for minorities. My upbringing was enriched by a brother, three and a half years my junior, contributing to a dynamic and educational family environment.

My academic journey began with an undergraduate degree in Psychology and a master's in social work. Post-graduation, I swiftly obtained certification as a marriage counselor and commenced my career as a play therapist for children.

My professional trajectory took a significant turn as I served as a psychiatric social worker at the Watts Health Center in Los Angeles, California. This experience was a precursor to my pursuit of further education, where I earned a master's in health services administration. The rigorous training instilled in me a deep understanding of structure, process, and outcome – principles that I integrated into my professional and personal life.

Leveraging my expertise in mental health and hospital administration, I assumed roles of increasing responsibility, overseeing psychiatry, social services, strategic planning, developmental disability, and hospital departments. An innovative blend of mental health knowledge and administrative acumen characterized my leadership.

My early life in the family funeral home business shaped my understanding of human behavior. Observing people navigate the complexities of grief and loss ignited my passion for psychology and profoundly influenced my personality development. These experiences, coupled with academic training, honed my ability to empathize, listen without judgment, and understand the diverse journeys of individuals.

In my role at the Watts Health Center, conducting mental status exams was enlightening, allowing me insights into the causes of my patients' struggles. This experience was not only professionally enriching but also provided valuable life lessons.

My career and life experiences have influenced every decision and action. I have diligently applied the knowledge acquired through my education to my life, ensuring that I learn from others' experiences and avoid repeating their mistakes.

The culmination of my journey is the inspiration behind this book, encouraged by friends, relatives, and colleagues who recognized the value in the unique parenting approach I employed with my two daughters, who have exceeded all my expectations. This book is a testament to the amalgamation of years of knowledge, experience, and purposeful parenting.

www.ingramcontent.com/pod-product-compliance
Lightning Source LLC
Chambersburg PA
CBHW062142280426
43673CB00072B/117